Carl Goldmark, Siegfried Lipiner, Gustav Kobbé

Merlin

An Opera in Three Acts

Carl Goldmark, Siegfried Lipiner, Gustav Kobbé

Merlin
An Opera in Three Acts

ISBN/EAN: 9783743696723

Hergestellt in Europa, USA, Kanada, Australien, Japan

Cover: Foto ©Thomas Meinert / pixelio.de

Weitere Bücher finden Sie auf **www.hansebooks.com**

LIBRETTO BY

SIEGFRIED LIPINER.

MUSIC BY

CARL GOLDMARK.

TRANSLATED BY GUSTAV KOBBÉ,

NEW YORK 1886.

Copyrighted in 1886.

CHARACTERS.

ARTHUR, King of Brittany. - - - - - - BARITONE.

GEINEVERE, his Wife, (dumb character), - - - - ———

MODRED, his nephew, ⎫ ⎧ - - TENOR.
GAWAIN, ⎪ ⎪ - BARITONE.
 ⎬ Knights of the Round Table, ⎨
LANCELOT, ⎪ ⎪ - - BARITONE.
MERLIN, ⎭ ⎩ - TENOR.

VIVIEN, ... SOPRANO.

BEDIVERE, a Knight, - - - - - - - BASS.

GLENDOWER, Steward of the Castle, - - - - - BASS.

THE FAY MORGANA, - - - - - - - ALTO.

THE DEMON, - - - - - - - - - BASS.

KNIGHTS, WARRIORS, MAIDENS, WOMEN, SPIRITS.

The Scene is laid in Wales near the Capitol.

SYNOPSIS OF PLOT.

The libretto of Merlin is the work of Siegfried Lipiner. It is in three acts in verse. The plot is as follows: The Devil, in order to beget a race which will drive all goodness out of the world, has forced the purest virgin on earth into a union with him. The fruit of this union is Merlin. But his mother's purity prevails in Merlin's character, and hence, instead of furthering the Devil's schemes, he combats them. He becomes one of the Knights of the Round Table. Through his supernatural gifts he is enabled to give victory to King Arthur over his heathen enemies. Combatting Merlin is the Devil through the agency of a Demon whom Merlin holds enslaved. The Demon learns through the all-wise woman, the Fay Morgana, that Merlin will lose his power if he should become enamored of a woman. How Merlin's fall is accomplished and how he is saved from perdition by the sacrifice of the very woman through whom the Demon hoped to bring about the seer's ruin are the main points of the story.

The characters in Merlin are as follows:

Arthur, King of the Britons.
Ginevra, his wife.
Modred, his nephew.
Gawain, Lancelot, Merlin, Viviane, Knights of the Round Table.
Bedwyr, a Knight.
Glendower, gatekeeper at the castle.
The Fay Morgana.
The Demon.
Knights, warriors, virgins, women, sprites.

AT KING ARTHUR'S CASTLE.

The action plays in Wales, near the capital. The scene of the first act is laid before King Arthur's castle. Lancelot brings ill tidings from the fray. Through treachery the foe has surrounded King Arthur's host. Unless Merlin aids all is lost. "Where is Merlin?" asks Lancelot of Glendower. Just then the strains of the seer's harp are heard from within the castle. Soon he appears at the castle gate. He checks Lancelot's speech, for he has divined what has happened Lancelot is bidden to return to the king with the message to stand firm and victory will surely be his. Lancelot hastily departs while Glendower enters the castle.

Merlin summons the Demon who appears in a fiery cloud. The seer commands his slave to wrap the enemy in blinding clouds and then to lead him astray with treacherously flickering lights. At the Demon's invocation, mists rise, form themselves into clouds and pass by, and will-o'-the-wisps float over the scene. Merlin then departs. The Demon curses the fate that makes him an evil one, the slave of the seer in the cause of righteousness. He summons the Fay Morgana, and from her learns that Merlin's powers will wane as soon as his thoughts are sullied by mundane lusts. He hastens away to entice into Merlin's presence, Viviane, the beautiful virgin of the forest spring. Martial music is heard. The host of King Arthur, victorious through Merlin, returns. There is a procession and the visitors are greeted by Ginevra and the populace with great rejoicing. Merlin lets his eyes run over the ranks of knights and points to Bedwyr as the traitor. Forced by the seer's power, the knight confesses his treachery. Then Merlin, as though inspired, sweeps his fingers over his harp's strings and intones a song of victory. Suddenly Viviane's voice is heard, In her swift pursuit of a deer she comes upon the concourse. Standing upon a high rock, with bow and arrow in her hand and surrounded by her virgins, she looks down upon the scene. Descending, she addresses Merlin. The seer's demeanor shows him impressed with her rare beauty. But, as though to shield himself against its influence, he roughly repulses her. In plaintive tones she begs him not to repulse her. His features have been reflected by the spring near which she dwells since she first saw him as he passed by in a procession of knights and warriors. Merlin, as though dazed by her beauty, covers his face with his hands.

SYNOPSIS OF PLOT.

The King hands a wreath of oak leaves to Viviane, that with it she crown Merlin. As she joyfully approaches the seer, he seems to awaken to a sense of danger. He bids her depart, and seizing his harp begins again to chant the song of victory. But his harp remains mute under his touch. "Depart evil one," he calls to Viviane. Incensed by his harshness, she hastens away, vowing that she will bring him to her feet. The King himself crowns Merlin. Amid rejoicing over the victory, the act closes.

THE MAGIC GARDEN.

The scene of the second act is laid in Merlin's magic garden. In the middle background are groups of trees beyond which the ocean gleams. To the right are high trees, rose bushes and a grassy seat. In the left foreground is a richly ornamented temple. It is a sunny afternoon. Modred, Bedwyr and several knights enter. Bedwyr disguised as a monk. They plot to seize the crown for Modred during King Arthur's absence on foreign conquest. Arthur, Gawain, Lancelot and numerous knights and warriors enter. Lancelot accuses Modred and his fellow-conspirators of treason. Swords are drawn, but the King interferes and appeals to Merlin, who joined the group. Merlin declares that Modred is free of guilt. So much already have his thoughts of Viviane weakened his powers of divination.

All except Merlin depart. He having gazed upon them, ascends several of the steps leading to the temple. At first lost in contemplation of the sanctuary, his thoughts are soon again with Viviane, and turning from the Temple he departs wrapt in contemplation. The Demon enters. He has been enticing Viviane thither. She soon comes into the garden. Approaching the temple she bids the gate open. It swings back, disclosing an altar upon which lies a veil. The Demon enters and brings out the veil to Viviane. She playfully tosses it upwards. It remains floating in the air emitting a soft radiance. Spirit voices are heard. A fountain suddenly gushes up from among the rose-bushes, and rose-colored mists float over the scene. Out of the fountain spring the water sprites, from the mists the air sprites, from the earth the earth sprites, from the rose-bushes the flower-sprites; and, finally after the dance of the sprites there is seen on the ocean, in a shell drawn by dolphins, the Queen of the Mermaids surrounded by her subjects.

Merlin comes upon the scene. Viviane seeing him, starts back with a cry. The sprites vanish. The veil falls upon a bush. When he hears that she tossed it into the air he is alarmed. Had she veiled herself with it, he explains, the lovely garden would have been changed into a howling wilderness. She turns to go her way; he calls her tenderly back and draws her gently toward him. A rhapsodical love scene follows, and, as the sun sets, Merlin and Viviane are sitting upon the grassy slope in each other's embrace, gazing enraptured into each other's eyes. There is a sudden tumult Glendower's voice is heard calling for Merlin. Modred and his followers have overpowered the King's adherents. Merlin now realizes that his passion for Viviane had rendered him powerless to divine Modred's fell purpose. He tries to conquer his rapture for her and depart to Glendower's aid. Viviane, in a paroxysm of rage and grief, seizes the fatal veil and throws it over Merlin. There is a terrific crash of thunder. Only the temple remains. Where the garden bloomed there is a dreary waste of rocks. Merlin is seen chained with fiery, glowing chains to a huge rock. The moon shines brightly. On a rock opposite Merlin stands the Demon, mocking him. Viviane, with a shriek, falls to the ground.

The third act opens on the same scene. Thick clouds hang over the background, so that only the temple and a huge rock, forming at its foot a kind of stone bench, are seen. It is morning. Viviane, in a half-raised posture near the rock, laments her deed which has brought misfortune on Merlin. In a bright light the Fay Morgana rises from her subterranean dwelling. She has heard the plaint of Viviane, who has sunk down in slumber. The ensuing scene is charming. As the Fay Morgana addresses comforting words to Viviane, she smiles in her sleep. The Fay prophesies that at the critical moment when the destroyer of souls thinks his triumph complete, Merlin may be saved by a woman's sacrifice. To Viviane the Fay's presence and comforting words are a lovely dream. Morgana vanishes and Viviane awakens. Her maidens approach, chanting a brisk chorus. The clouds lift and Merlin chained to the rock is seen. Mocking sprites dance around him.

LAST SCENE OF ALL.

The tumult of the battle is heard. Lancelot rushes in to seek Merlin's aid. Modred has joined the Saxons and King Arthur is in danger. Merlin tugs desperately at his chains. For his

SYNOPSIS OF PLOT.

freedom he will pledge his soul to hell. "Be free!" shouts the demon. The chains fall. The scene changes back to the garden. Merlin rushes forth to the fray. "Victory is mine!" shouts the Demon. Viviane garlands herself with leaves and flowers, and with her maiden awaits Merlin's return. The tumult of battle subsides. A funeral march is heard. Victory has been won at the cost of Merlin's life. Viviane throws herself upon his bier. The dying seer clasps her to his breast. The Demon appears and claims Merlin as his own. Suddenly Viviane recalls her vision and the words of the dream-woman, that Merlin may be saved by a woman's sacrifice. Drawing a dagger she stabs herself to the heart and sinks into death with Merlin. The Demon foiled, sinks into the earth.

MERLIN.

ACT I.

(In the background, at the summit of a steep ascent on the left, King Arthur's Castle. A high gate in the middle, a smaller gate on either side. The main gate opens upon a terrace. Below it, a decorated tent surrounded by flowering plants. To the right, toward the background, rocks. In the distance, a view of Carleon, the Capitol. Whitsuntide; dawn as the curtain rises.)

SCENE FIRST.

(Enter LANCELOT from the right.)

Lancelot
(knocking at the gate.
Ho there! Glendower! Ope straightway!

Glendower
(appearing at a side gate.
Lancelot—you! How stands the fray?

Lancelot.
Unhappy day!

Glendower.
What do I hear!

Lancelot.
The worst that heroes have to fear:
The enemy had fled, complete his rout,
When suddenly we hear in the rear a shout.
We are surrounded—a traitor hath
Shown to the Saxons a hidden path!

Glendower.
The traitorous villain!

Lancelot.
The battle is lost,
The King in danger, captured our host.
If Merlin appear not to save the day,
Wise Merlin, our savior in many a fray—
Where is he now?

Glendower
(pointing toward the castle.
Hark! Hear'st not the sounds from his harp that arise?
I saw him—there kneels he, as lost in prayer,
And as inspired, he turns his eyes
Toward Heaven, as though to enter there;
At times like these the prophet seems to see
Into the future and its mystery.
That sacred power is his alone I ween.

Lancelot.
Him I must see!
(The main portal opens.

Glendower.
Behold him!
(Merlin, harp in hand, appears upon the terrace.)

Lancelot
(hastening toward him.
Merlin! Hear!

Merlin.
Be calm, for every thing I know.
Go! and to Arthur bear these words—
Thy hope is in thy heroes' swords,
Fight bravely! thou shalt route the foe!

MERLIN.

ERSTER AKT.

(Links schräg im Hintergrunde Artus' Burg. Hohes Mittelthor, kleinere Nebenthore. Vor dem Hauptthore eine Terrasse. Unterhalb derselben, von blühenden Gebüschen umgeben, ein geschmücktes Zelt. Rechts, gegen den Hintergrund zu, Felsen. In der Perspective Ausblick auf die Stadt Karleon. Pfingstzeit. Anfangs Morgendämmerung, dann heller Tag.)

ERSTE SCENE.

LANCELOT kommt von der Rechten, dann GLENDOWER.

Lancelot
(an's Thor klopfend.
Heda! Glendower! Aufgemacht!

Glendower
(aus einem Nebenthor kommend.
Lancelot — Du! Wie steht die Schlacht?

Lancelot
Unseliger Tag!

Glendower.
Was gibt's, sag an!

Lancelot.
Das Schlimmste, was ich melden kann:
Wir jubelten schon, schon floh der Feind,
Als plötzlich ein Haufe im Rücken erscheint;
Einer der Unsern — schnöder Verrath! —
Wies den Sachsen verborgenen Pfad!

Glendower.
Ha, schändlicher Bube!

Lancelot.
Wir sind umgangen,
Wir sind verloren, sind gefangen,
Rettet uns nicht vor Schmach und Tod
Der Eine, der Retter in jeglicher Noth —
Wo ist Merlin?

Glendower
(nach der Burg deutend.
Still! hörst du des Sehers Harfe klingen?
Ich sah ihn: dort kniet er, in Andacht versunken,
Aufblickt sein Aug', so feurig-trunken,
Als wollt' es in die Himmel dringen;
In solchen Stunden stör' ich ihn nicht,
Da leuchtet am hellsten sein Seherlicht,
Die heil'ge Kraft, die ihm allein verlieh'n —

Lancelot.
Ich muss ihn seh'n!
(Das Mittelthor öffnet sich.

Glendower.
Da ist er!

Merlin
(war, die Harfe in der Hand, auf der Terrasse erschienen.

Lancelot
(ihm rasch entgegen.
Hör'! — Merlin!

Merlin.
Sei ruhig, alles weiss ich schon.
Geh' — und dem König sollst du melden:
Fest halt' er Stand mit seinen Helden,
Der hehrste Sieg wird Euch zum Lohn!

MERLIN.

Lancelot.

Hail, noble seer! Forthwith I go.
Thy word will be fulfilled I know.
We'll fight inspired by hope of victory.
If thou art with us, none can conquer thee.

(Exit Lancelot to the right, Glendower into the castle.)

SCENE SECOND.

MERLIN, DEMON.

Merlin

(Rests his harp against the tent on the left and comes forward).
Demon!

Demon.

(Appears in a fiery cloud)
Here am I!

Merlin.

Haste to the fight!
Cover the Saxons with clouds and with night!
Let blindness strike the heathenish foe!
The cross shall conquer!

Demon.

I swear it, No.
Accursed cross! Accursed yoke!

Merlin.

In the name of the Father—

Demon.

Dread Merlin! be still!

Merlin.

Haste! Gather the clouds! Wilt thou?

Demon.

I will!
Hither! Hither! From far and near!
Mists of the Moors, your Master here!
Weave yourselves, wind round the heathen swarm—
'Round head and foot, 'round eye and arm!

(Chorus of spirits invisible.)

Soon will we weave around, soon will we wind around:
Master of hell, thou our praises shall sound!

(Mists rise, shape themselves into clouds and float past.)

Merlin.

And send to the foe, while in darkness he gropes,
Send him marsh-lanterns, traitorous hopes,—
Glimmers beguiling, and blinding his glance!

Demon.

Ye Will-o'-the-whisps! be your mission dread
With capering paces and glittering head,
To compass the foe in your treacherous dance!

(Chorous of Ghosts, invisible.)

We caper, we whizz, we encircle him round;
Master of hell, thou our praises shall sound!

(Will-o'-the-whisps glimmer in the bushes and vanish.)

Merlin.

'Tis well, my slave: your master obey;
And turn for the Cross the tide of the fray!

(Exit.)

Demon.

Acursed magician; Oh bitter pain!
How long wilt thou bind me with slav'ry's chain?
How long must I serve his fiendish race?
As a child he held me in bondage base;
Was the plant of evil about to flower,
A glance from him would blast its power;
The past and the future to him are known,
The powers of hell he's made his own—
And me he could shatter at any hour:
I know not how to withstand his power!

(Silent, then weirdly whispering.)

MERLIN.

Lancelot.
Dank, edler Seher! Ich eile fort:
Nie trog dein heilig Seherwort!
Wir wollen kühn auf's Neu' zum Kampfe
  geh'n!
Bist du mit uns, wer mag uns wider-
  steh'n?
(Lancelot ab nach der Rechten, Glendower in die
Burg.

ZWEITE SCENE.

MERLIN. DAEMON.

Merlin
(lehnt seine Harfe an das Zelt links und tritt
vor.
Dämon!

Daemon
(erscheint plötzlich in einer feurigen Wolke.
Hier bin ich!

Merlin.
Fort in die Schlacht!
Hülle die Sachsen in Wolken und Nacht!
Mit Blindheit schlag' das heidnische
  Heer!
Hell siege das Kreuz!

Daemon.
Nein, nimmermehr!
Verhasstes Kreuz! verwünschtes Joch!

Merlin
(ruhig.
Und dienst du ihm knirschend, so dienst
  du doch!
Im Namen des Vaters!

Daemon.
Verfluchter, sei still!

Merlin.
Auf! sammle die Wolken! Willst du?

Daemon.
Ich will! —
Herbei, herbei, von nah' und fern:
Dünste des Moors, höret den Herrn!
Umwindet, umwebet den heidnischen
  Schwarm —
Um Haupt und Fuss, um Aug' und
  Arm!

Geisterchor
(unsichtbar.
Bald ist er umwunden, bald is er umwo-
  ben:
Meister der Hölle, du wirst uns loben!
(Nebeldünste erheben sich, ballen sich zu Wolken und ziehen vorbei.)

Merlin.
Und sende dem Feind in's lähmende
  Dunkel,
Send' ihm der Flämmchen tückisch Ge-
  funkel,
Trügend verlock' ihn der schwirrende
  Glanz.

Daemon.
Irrwische! Irrwische! naht euch verstoh-
  len,
Mit brennenden Köpfen, mit hüpfenden
  Sohlen,
Schlingt um die Heiden den tückischen
  Tanz!

Geisterchor
(unsichtbar.
Wir hüpfen, wir schwirren, von unten,
  von oben:
Meister der Hölle, du sollst uns loben!
(Irrlichter funkeln im Gebüsch auf und schwei-
fen vorüber.)

Merlin.
Wohl! Du kannst geh'n: es ist voll-
  bracht;
So bring es denn Heil! — Nun fort in die
  Schlacht!
(Geht ab.

Daemon.
Verfluchter Zauberer! verhasster Zwang!
Wie lange noch knechtest du mich, wie
  lang'?
So muss ich ihm dienen, dem Teufels-
  sohn!
Da er noch Kind war, dient' ich ihm
  schon;
Wollt' ich ein Werk des Unheils begin-
  nen,
Sein offner Blick trieb mich von hin-
  nen!
Vergangenes, Künftiges ist ihm bewusst,
Die Hölle zwingt er nach seiner Lust —
Und ob er mich in Trümmer bricht:
Wie ihm zu wehren, weiss ich nicht!
(Stillschweigen, dann schauerlich leise.

Where deep a fiery river flows
A woman dwells, who all things knows.
Within her crystal palace bright
She sees the swift hours in their flight.
Whe whole wide world one weapon fierce
Alone affords his heart to pierce:
'Tis known to you, Morgana Fay!
Will you my vengeance show the way!
(Impressively.)
 You, begotten of the higher
 Powers of water and of fire,
 Mistress you of gramarye,
 Fay Morgana, list to me!
 Forth from your crystal palace hall
 Haste, Morgana, at my call!

 By the spring of darkness dread,
 By the magic's fountain head,
 By the seething, bubbling water,
 Of which you are the radiant daughter:
 By the fountain of thy birth,
 Fay Morgana, rise to earth!

(A steaming spring suddenly bursts forth from the ground; a fiery sheen diffuses itself over the stage. Out of the spring rises Morgana, with a diadem, in a fiery red tunic draped with a green veil.)

THIRD SCENE.

THE DEMON, MORGANA.

Morgana.

Who calls me?

Demon.

Hear, Queen Morgana! list to me!

Morgana.

In you old Merlin's slave I see!

Demon.

You hither to mock me I did not call!

Morgana.

Demon—whom would'st thou enthrall?

Demon.

The Prince of Darkness once indulged the passion
To have a son who should make sin the fashion;
The purest maid he forced to be his queen,
And Merlin was the offspring thus foreseen.
Though like his father he in magic powers,
Our hopes, alas, are false, undone we are;
Endowed by us, yet will he not be ours—
For bright o'er him shines his mother's star!
(Hotly.
Know you him well, know you his heavenly mien?
Know you his seer's power,—supernal might
By which the tempter's put to flight?
Great Queen! O answer, answer now!

Morgana.

Noble Merlin! blest art thou!

Demon.

Speak, how may I vanquish him?

Morgana.

Noble Merlin! blest art thou!
Hark! I hear his harp resounding
Sacred tones of holy rite.

Demon.

Yea, his mother's peace and rest
Enter with each note his breast;—
Speak, how may I conquer him?

Morgana.

An! I see your mind is sounding
Depths of his mysterious might;—

Demon.

Were that splendor in his eyes
Quenched, a victor I would rise—
Speak, how can I blind his view?

Morgana.

Merlin! Merlin! Woe to you!
Pure must be the hand to sweep
O'er that wondrous instrument;
Conquer every lustful bent
Or the Harp will silence keep;

MERLIN.

Es lebt ein Weib, dem alles kund:
Auf heissen Stromes tiefsten Grund,
In ihrem Schlosse von Krystall,
Schaut sie das weite Welten all.
Ist in der ganzen weiten Welt
Nur eine Waffe, die ihn fällt:
Kund ist's Morgana, deinem Geist! —
Ob du mir Rath und Rache weisst?

(Feierlich.
Du, erschaffen und beseelt,
Als sich Glut und Flut vermählt,
Du, des Zaubers Meisterin,
Fee Morgana, Seherin:
Aus dem Strom, den du erkoren,
Sei beschworen, sei beschworen!

Bei dem Quell der Finsterniss,
Der der Erde Schooss zerriss,
Bei dem siedend heissen Quell,
D'raus du aufstiegst leuchtend hell:
Bei der Flut, die dich geboren:
Sei beschworen, sei beschworen!

(Eine heisse, von wallenden Dämpfen umwogte Springquelle scheint aus der Erde hervorzubrechen; ein feuerrother Glanz ergiesst sich von ihr über die Bühne. Aus der Quelle erhebt sich Morgana, ein Diadem auf dem Haupte, in feurigrothem Gewand, von grünem Schleier umflattert.)

DRITTE SCENE.

DAEMON. MORGANA.

Morgana.

Wer ruft mir?

Daemon.

Hör' mich, Morgana, Königin!

Morgana.

Bist du der Sclave des Merlin?

Daemon.

Nicht mich zu höhnen, beschwor ich dich her!

Morgana.

Rede — was ist dein Begehr?

Daemon.

Der Hölle Fürst wollt' einen Sohn erzeugen,
Dem Heil zu wehren und die Welt zu beugen;
Die reinste Jungfrau zwang er mit Gewalt —
Ein Sohn entspross: ein Wunder an Gestalt,
Dem Vater gleich an Zauberkraft und Stärke;
Doch ach! er trog die Hoffnung uns'res Herrn:
Die Hölle zwingt er zu des Himmels Werke —
Denn heilig strahlt ob ihm der Mutter Stern!

(Heftig.
Kennst du ihn wohl und seinen heiligen Sinn?
Kennst seine Seherkraft — das Himmelslicht,
Das des Versuchers Künste bricht?
O rede, rede, Königin!

Morgana.

Selig bist du, Held Merlin!

Daemon.

Rede, wie vernicht ich ihn?

Morgana.

Selig bist du, Held Merlin!
Deine Harfe hör' ich klingen,
Heilig rührt der Töne Macht —

Daemon.

Heil'ger Mutter Fried' und Ruh'
Weht ihm aus den Tönen zu —
Sprich, wie zwing' ich heil'gen Sinn?

Morgana.

Deine Blicke seh' ich dringen
Durch geheimnissvolle Nacht —

Daemon.

Ist der *Blick* nur ihm entrafft,
Spott' ich seiner Zauberkraft —
Sprich, wie blend' ich Sehersinn?

Morgana.

Weh', dir, wehe, Held Merlin! —
Nur in heilig-reinster Hand
Tönt das Wundersaitenspiel;
Heisser Wünsche eitlem Ziel
Sei der Seher abgewandt! —

MERLIN.

If the Harp should e'er refuse
To respond unto your muse,
'Twill thy seer's power undo;
And then, Merlin, woe to you,
   (The light grows dimmer—Morgana slowly sinks.)

Demon.

When, Ah! when will't vanish—tell!

Morgana

Spare me!

Demon.

By the Devil's throne
Let the evil power be known!

Morgana.

Spare me!

Demon.

'Tis the hope of hell!

Morgana.

Merlin! Merlin! woe to thee!
From your holy service turning,
And for lustful pleasure yearning,
For a maid your heart is burning—
Merlin! Merlin! woe to thee.
                       (vanishes.

Demon.

A maid! A maid! 'Tis thus I shall be freed,
The loveliest of maids to him I'll lead,
At last! at last! my hope is bounding
No more I hear thy Harp resounding;
Thy seer's glance shall change to-night,
Vain be thy boasted magic's might;
And when I once through craft infernal
Dethrone thee, thine shall be eternal
Ruin. By no power withholden,
I'll keep the in my power enfolden;
Thus for my shame I'll thee requite.
   (He vanishes. The sun rises. The gates of the castle are thrown open. There is much coming and going of retainers. Trumpets are heard.

SCENE FOUTRH.

(Glendower; Girls; Women; Populace entering from all directions. Lancelot.)

Glendower.

Hear you those trumpets! The King has fought

And conquered, and treason base has come to naught,
Most fortunate day!

Chorus.

Long shall live the name
Of Arthur! Great will be his fame!—

Women from the Castle.

They come, they come, see how the light
Plays brilliantly o'er their weapons bright!
The colors are flying, the trumpets resounding!

Lancelot

               (enters from the right.
Our pæans joyous they are sounding;
That was a battle—man to man!
The King was fighting far in the van!
Ehe foe hemmed us in through treachery base,
Threatening our valiant host to efface!
When lo, as lightning in clouds appears,
Our hero, Merlin, among the spears!
And struck with dismay the ranks of the foe
Fall back, as the hunter's prey is laid low.
Felled are our enemies! Ye see
The King's green wreath of Victory!
            (enters the castle with Glendower.

Chorus of Bards and Warriors.

He comes, he comes, our noble King!
His sword and lance are red,
With blood of hostile dead;
With every blow and thrust
A foeman bit the dust!
He comes, he comes, our noble King!
Hail, Victor brave!

Women and Men.

            (The women strewing roses.
Roses red, roses sweet
Scattering at your feet
Joyously you we greet
Noble King serene.

Wenn der Harfe Ton verklingt:
Weh' dir, wehe, Held Merlin!
All dein Schauen ist dahin,
Und dein Seherlicht versinkt.
<small>Der Schein wird matter, Morgana versinkt langsam.)</small>

Daemon.

Wann versinkt es — rede: wann?

Morgana.

Lass mich!

Daemon.

Bei der Hölle Thoren:
Sei beschworen! sei beschworen!

Morgana.

Lass mich!

Daemon.

Weile, künd' es an!

Morgana.

Weh' dir, wehe, Held Merlin!
Bist zu heil'gem Dienst gesendet,
Hast zu Wonnen dich gewendet:
Denn *ein Weib* hat dich geblendet —
Weh' dir, wehe, Held Merlin!
<small>(Verschwindet.</small>

Daemon.

Ein Weib! ein Weib! Nun hab' ich
  Waff' und Wehr!
Das schönste Weib, — ich sah's — ich
  lock' es her!
Triumph! Triumph! es wird gelingen!
Die heil'ge Harfe wird verklingen,
Dein Seherlicht versinkt in Nacht!
Dann wahre deine Zaubermacht!
Wenn ich sie einmal dir entwunden,
Dich binde, wie du mich gebunden:
Nicht kurze Pein soll mir genügen,
In ew'gen Fesseln sollst du liegen —
Ich raste nicht, bis ich's vollbracht!
<small>(Er verschwindet. — Die Sonne geht auf. Die Thore der Burg werden geöffnet. Bewegtes Treiben. — Trompetenstösse immer näher.)</small>

VIERTE SCENE

<small>(Glendower, Mädchen Frauen, Volk von allen Seiten kommend, gleich darauf Lancelot.)</small>

Glendower.

Hört ihr es klingen? Der König naht!
Zu Schanden ward der schändliche Verrath!
Glückseliger Tag!

Chor.

Heil der Botschaft! Heil!
Der hehrste Sieg ward uns zu Theil!

Frauen aus dem Schlosse.

Wo ist der König? Wo ist das Heer?

Volk
<small>(von rechts.</small>

Sie nahen, sie kommen: mit blinkender
  Wehr,
Mit fliegenden Fahnen, mit hellen Trompeten!

Lancelot.
<small>(kommt von rechts.</small>

Der Sachsen Macht, sie liegt zertreten!—
Das war ein Ringen, Mann an Mann!
Der König stritt uns Allen voran!
Da plötzlich erscheint, von Wolken umwallt,
Mitten im Feind des Sehers Gestalt;
Wir stürzen vor und jauchzen: Merlin!
Er schwang sein Schwert und stürmte
  dahin:
Ein Schrecken ergriff die feindlichen
  Reih'n,
Sie wichen, sie flohen — wir hieben ein.—
Seht, wie das Haupt des Königs glänzt,
Von grünem Siegerkranz bekränzt!
<small>(Ab in die Burg mit Glendower.</small>

Chor der Barden und Krieger.

Er naht, der Fürst des Sieges naht!
Und Schwert und Lanze raucht,
In Feindesblut getaucht;
Und wo sein Schild erschien,
Dort sank ein Held dahin.
So führt er kühn von That zu That —
Der Fürst des Siegs!

Frauen und Maenner.
<small>(Frauen Rosen streuend.</small>

Rosen, all ihr süssen,
Eilt zu seinen Füssen;
Lass dich froh begrüssen,
König, stark und kühn!

Frauen.

Heil dir, hehre
Schaar der Ehre!
Schild und Speere
Kränzt mit jungem Maiengrün!

MERLIN.

Men and Women.

Hail ye fearless
Victors peerless;
Shield and weapons
Let us wreathe with oaken green.
(Some of the women wreathe with flowers the shields and spears of the warriors.)

II.

He comes! he comes, our noble King! etc.,

Men and Women.

Let the foliage oaken,
Be the victor's token,
Wreathe their shields and lances,
Joyous be our mien!

Women and Men.

Hail ye fearless
Victors peerless!
Shield and weapons
Let us wreathe with oaken green.
He comes, he comes, our noble King!
His sword and lance are red
With blood of hostile dead;
With every blow and thrust
A foeman bit the dust!
He comes, he comes, our noble King!
Hail, Victor brave!

SCENE FIFTH.

(Arthur, Gawain, Bedivere, Modred, with many knights and warriors, come during the following choruses from the right. Arthur is crowned with a garland of oak. Guinevere comes with her woman out of the castle, led by Lancelot. Glendower follows.

Chorus of Women.

Crowned he is with oaken leaves
At his feet are flowers:
And the sun of morning bright
Radiance o'er him showers!
Shameless treason came to naught
For the right was ours.
Over foe and traitor both
Triumphed Christian powers!

Chorus of Warriors

(at the same time.
Ha! that was a warriors' dance!
Fearful was our meeting,
To the morning's radiance
Gladly give we greeting!
Shameless treason came to nought
For the right was ours!
Over foe and traitor both
Triumphed Christian Powers!

Chorus of Populace.

Hail King Arthur! Victor hail!
May you o'er all foes prevail!

Arthur.

I greet you, my people, and give you thanks;
And you, brave Knights of the Round Table;
Right firm in battle were your ranks!
E'en when a traitor despicable
Did lead against your ranks unbroken,
Strong as the trees in forests oaken
The foeman's band, 'gainst King and land
He raised his vile and trait'rous hand!

Chorus.

Curse him! His vile and trait'rous hand
Was raised against his King and land!

Arthur.

But where is he, the noble one,
By whom alone the day was won!
He smote the foes with blinded sight—
They broke their ranks and fled in fright!
Where's Merlin, the first in council and war,
The seer, the bard, whom the foe abhor?

Chorus.

Through him to us the victory came;
Hail, Merlin, seer! Praise his name.

Arthur.

Now lead him hither; hasten, women all,
A wreath to weave for him of freshest green,

Maenner.

Heilig-hehre
Heldenehre,
Dich verkläre
Rosenpracht und Maiengrün!
(Ein Theil der Frauen bekränzt Schilde und Lanzen der Krieger.)

II.

Er naht! Der Fürst des Sieges naht
u. s. w.

Frauen und Maenner.

Schmücket Schild und Lanze
Mit dem Eichenkranze!
In des Tages Glanze
Mag die Freude blüh'n!

Frauen.

Heil dir, hehre
Schaar der Ehre!
Schild und Speere
Kränzt mit jungem Maiengrün.

Maenner.

Heilig-hehre
Heldenehre,
Dich verkläre
Rosenpracht und Maiengrün!
Er naht, der Fürst des Sieges naht —
u. s. w.

FUENFTE SCENE.

(Artus, Gawein, Bedwyr, Modred mit vielen Rittern und Kriegern kommen während des folgenden Chores von der Rechten. Artus' Haupt ist mit grünem Eichenkranz geschmückt. Ginevra kommt mit ihren Frauen aus der Burg, von Lancelot geführt. Glendower folgt.)

Chor der Frauen.

Um das Haupt den Eichenkranz,
Rosen Euch zu Füssen:
Mögt ihr so des Morgens Glanz
Immerda begrüssen!
Was Euch Tücke zugedacht,
Wurde doch zu Schanden,
Herrlich ist aus heisser Schlacht
Euch der Sieg erstanden!

Chor der Krieger
(zugleich.

Hei, das war ein Waffentanz!
Mussten's theuer büssen!
Lass dich denn, o Morgenglanz,
Doppelt froh begrüssen!
Was uns Tücke zugedacht,
Wurde doch zu Schanden;
Und aus wundenreicher Schlacht
Ist der Sieg erstanden!

Chor des Volkes.

Heil dem König! Heil dem Heer!
Heil des Tages Glanz und Ehr'!

Artus.

Gruss Euch, ihr Guten, und frohen Dank!
Dank dir, du tapfre Tafelrunde,
Voll Muth und Treue sonder Wank!
Dank allem Heer zur glücklichen Stunde!
Ihn aber, der das Heer geschändet,
Ihn, der von schnödem Gold verblendet,
Verkauft, verrathen Fürst und Land:
Ihn treffe Gottes Rächerhand!

Chor.

Fluch ihm! Ihn treffe Gottes Hand,
Der schnöd verrathen Fürst und Land!

Artus.

Wo aber ist Er, der hohe Mann,
Der einzig heut den Sieg gewann,
Der unsre Feinde mit Blindheit schlug,
Der Schrecken in ihre Reihen trug:
Wo ist er, der Erste im Rath, im Feld —
Merlin, mein Seher, mein Barde, mein Held?

Chor.

Durch ihn ward uns der Sieg verlieh'n:
Heil ihm, dem Seher! Heil Merlin!

Artus.

Führt ihn heran! — Ihr aber, Frauen, eilt:
Zum Kranze windet mir das schönste Grün!
Dem einzigen Manne, edel, gross und kühn,
Sei er als schwacher Dank ertheilt!
(Einige Frauen ab.)

MERLIN.

For him our bravest one, the lordliest of mien;
His we ordain this festival.
(Several women exeunt. Merlin is led in by several knights. Arthur hastening to meet him.)
O Merlin, Merlin! Faithful friend,
What love and valor in my hero blend!
(He seizes his hand and gazes lovingly into his eyes.)
Yes! strong am I to bear whate'er betides,
Danger and want and spite are naught to me
While eyes like yours are watching land and sea,
And while your friendship in my heart abides!
(He points to the multitude.
Not I alone—See all these people here:
Your thankful praise they bring from far and near!
Gaze in mine eyes and read my sorrow's end,
That in you, Merlin, I may claim a friend!

Merlin.

My noble King, this praise is undeserved
Your army 'twas; the ranks that never swerved!
(At the last words he scans the ranks of the knights till his eyes rest on Bedivere.)

Merlin.

Your name now tell me?

Bedivere.

Bedivere.

Merlin.

'Twas you!

Chorus.

What says he?

Merlin.

Traitor I know you.

Bedivere.

A liar you!

Merlin
(Calmly.
Your guilty face a traitor vile does show you
Look in my eyes, and frank be your reply!
You are the traitor! Speak—Can you deny!

Bedivere
(drawing back.
Away!

Merlin.

Confess!

Bedivere.

Your charges I despise.

Merlin.

Have you not done it? Look me in the eyes!

Bedivere.

Within your eyes burns devilish fire!

Merlin.

Confess!

Bedivere.

Away! You are in the evil one's pay,
Through you he seeks me to betray!
Here is my sword! now feel my ire!

Merlin.

Speak calmly—can you it deny?
(He lays both hands on Bedivere's shoulder.
Look up and answer.

Bedivere
(About to attack him looks involuntarily into Merlin's eyes and drops his sword.)
'Twas I! 'Twas I!
(sinks down.

Full Chorus.

'Tis magic; unto him is known,
Each thought as though it were his own!

Chorus of the Populace.

O mighty Merlin! seer, prophet clear;
Shame to the traitor! Woe to him here.

MERLIN.

Merlin
(wird von mehreren Rittern herangeführt.

Artus
(ihm entgegeneilend.
Merlin, mein Freund! mein theurer Held!
Wo wär' ein Dank dein würdig in der Welt?
(Er ergreift seine Hand und sieht ihm liebevoll in's Auge.)
Ja! stark ertrag' ich, was mein Herz bedrückt:
Gefahr und Noth und schnöder Tücke Macht —
Da solch ein Aug' ob meinem Haupte wacht,
Da Freundestreu mein Innerstes erquickt.
(Er zeigt ihm die versammelte Menge.
Dir dank' ich nicht! — O sieh' dies Volk ringsum:
Sein jauchzend Herz, das sei dein Dank und Ruhm!
Sieh mir in's Aug', und lies das Glück darin,
Dass mir ein Freund gegeben, wie Merlin!

Merlin.
Mein edler Fürst — ich bin nicht Lobes werth,
Dir half dein Heer, dir half dein starkes Schwert!
(Sein Blick durchläuft bei den letzten Worten die Reihen der Ritter und trifft nun auf Bedwyr.)

Merlin.
Wie ist dein Name?

Bedwyr.
Bedwyr.

Merlin.
Du warst's!

Chor.
Was sagt er?

Merlin.
Du hast verrathen!

Bedwyr.
Ha, Lügner du!

Merlin
(ruhig.
In deinen Blicken liegen deine Thaten! —
Sich' mir in's Auge — sieh mich offen an!
Willst du mir leugnen? Sprich — hast du's gethan?

Bedwyr
(zurückweichend.
Hinweg!

Merlin.
Gesteh'!

Bedwyr.
Nichts hab' ich zu gesteh'n!

Merlin.
Hast du's gethan? Kannst du in's Aug' mir sehen?

Bedwyr.
In deinem Aug' brennt teuflische Glut!

Merlin.
Gesteh'!

Bedwyr
(das Schwert ziehend.
Hinweg! Du bist mit dem Bösen im Bund!
Er lügt durch deinen Lügenmund!
Hinweg! sonst trinkt mein Schwert dein Blut!

Merlin.
Sei ruhig! Hast du es gethan!
(Er legt ihm beide Hände auf die Schultern.
Blick auf und Rede!

Bedwyr
(will auf ihn eindringen und blickt dabei unwillkürlich in sein Auge. Das Schwert entfällt ihm.)
Ich hab's gethan!
(Er sinkt nieder.

Voller Chor.
O Grauen! Alles ist ihm kund,
Er blickt in jedes Herzens Grund!

Chor des Volkes.
O grosser Seher, mächtiger Merlin!
Schmach dem Verräther! Fluch über ihn!

Chorus of Warriors.

Oh shame, disgrace, death be the due
Of him who sought to betray the true !
(Merlin steps to the tent and grasps his harp.)

Arthur.

Lead him away ! Death for his crime !
(Bedivere is led away ; a fresh wreath of oak-leaves is brought to Arthur.)

Merlin
(raising his harp.
Unhappy hour that saw the crime !
Most shame-begetting day in time !
Let us our hearts with faith imbuing
Uplift our hands our oath renewing :
Let it unite us in one band :
" True to King Arthur ! True to our land "!

Chorus of Knights.

This oath unites us in one band :
" True to King Arthur ! True to our land !

Merlin

(intoning his harp as though inspired.
To you, my King, I sound my praise ;
You, rich in wounds and in glory,
The Northern ice the Southern sun
Know of your fame the story !
Hostile armies against us are rushing
Like waves of a stormy roaring flood !
You come, the angry billows hushing ;
'Gainst you they dash and are subdued

Chorus.

To you King Arthur sounds our praise !

Merlin.

To you I sound my Highland praise
Amid your crags eternal !
Although the tempest on you plays
You stand in vigor vernal.
Vain and weak their strife to frighten
And quell my warrior whose blows are so strong,
Smiling with joy when wild heavens lighten,
And shouting when storms around you throng.

Chorus.

To you, our Highland praise, we sound!

Merlin.

Hail to you day of victory !

Vivien's Voice
(from behind the scenes.
Hallalee ! hallalee !
Deer, you may
Run away,
Yet you'll be my arrow's prey ;
You may flee
Fast and free,
Though you beat
Swift retreat
My sharp arrow too is fleet !
Hallalee ! hallalee !
Deer, you may
Run away,
Yet you'll be my arrow's prey !

SIXTH SCENE.

(During this song Vivien with bow and arrows in her hand appears with her maidens on a rock to the right. Noticing the gathering, she runs down into its midst. General commotion.)

Voices.

The Virgin of the Spring—the roving huntress free !

Vivien
(approaching Merlin.
I greet you, Merlin !—Tis none else than he.

Merlin
(regards her a while in silence.
Who are you ? and what seek you here ?
Do you not see the King is near ?
(Points to Arthur, to whom Vivien makes a deep obeisance. Severely.)
Why come you upon us with shout so loud ?

Vivien.

Are you to answer my question too proud ?
To you I surely need give no reply :
A deer—or was't a roe—I know not why

MERLIN

Chor der Krieger.
Ha, Schand' und Schmach, Fluch dem
  Verrath!
Mit seinem Blute sühn' er die That!

Merlin
(tritt an das Zelt und ergreift seine Harfe.

Artus.
Führt ihn hinweg! ihm wird sein Lohn!
(Bedwyr wird weggeführt; man bringt Artus
einen frischen Eichenkranz.)

Merlin
(seine Harfe erhebend.
O Schmach dem Tag, der Solches ge-
  seh'n!
In dieser Stunde, da dies gescheh'n,
Lasst uns, Ihr Tapfern, Ihr Getreuen,
Lasst uns den heil'gen Schwur erneuen:
Ruft und hebt zum Himmel die Hand:
Treue dem König! Treue dem Land!

Chor der Ritter.
Wir rufen und heben zum Himmel die
  Hand:
Treue dem König! Treue dem Land!

Merlin
(begeistert in die Saiten greifend.
Heil dir, mein König, Heil und Preis,
Du, reich an Wunden und Siegen!
Des Südlands Trift, des Nordlands Eis,
Sah deine Fahnen fliegen.
Brausend kommen die Völker gezogen,
Umfluten dein Volk mit wilder Macht:
Du kommst — du bändigst ihre Wogen,
Du mächtiger Wirbelwind der Schlacht!

Chor.
Heil dir, mein König, Heil dir und
  Preis!

Merlin.
Heil dir, mein Hochland, Preis und
  Heil,
In deiner Felsen Mitten!
Wie deine Felsen rauh und steil,
So stehst du, hart umstritten.
Brandend kommt das Meer gezogen,
Sie zu zerbrechen, wie müht es sich
  stark!
Aber zu Schanden werden die Wogen
An meines Hochlands felsigem Mark!

Chor.
Heil dir, mein Hochland! Preis dir
  und Heil!

Merlin.
Heil dir, o Tag, du Siegestag!......

Vivianes Stimme
(hinter der Bühne.
Hallali! hallali!
Hirschlein fein,
Streck' die Bein',
Bogen kommt doch hinterdrein;
Lauf geschwind,
Wie der Wind,
Wie ein Hauch,
Ueber'n Strauch:
Bogen, Bogen läuft ja auch!
Hallali! hallali!
Hirschlein fein,
Streck' die Bein',
Sieh dich vor,— schon bist du mein!

SECHSTE SCENE.

(Vorige. Viviane mit ihren Jungfrauen war
während ihres Gesanges, Pfeil und Bogen in der
linken Hand auf einem Felsen zur Rechten erschienen; jetzt bemerkt sie die Versammlung
und rennt mitten auf die Bühne herab. Allge-
meine Unruhe.)

Stimmen
(durcheinander.
Das Fräulein von der Quelle —die wilde
  Jägerin! —

Viviane
(auf Merlin zugehend.
Merlin! Er ist's Ich grüsse dich, Merlin!

Merlin
(sieht sie eine Weile schweigend an.
Wer bist du? und was suchst du hier?
Hier ist geheiligtes Revier!
(Auf den König weisend, vor welchem sich Vi-
viane tief verneigt, rauh:
Was drängst du dich so laut in diesen
  Kreis?

Viviane.
Wer Frauengruss nicht zu erwidern
  weiss:
Verdient der wohl, dass ich ihm Rede
  steh'?
Ein Hirschlein jagt' ich — oder war's
  ein Reh —

MERLIN.

Confused I stand—You gave so stern a look
That courage suddenly my heart forsook!
I know not of what deed I might be guilty
This arrow mine—

(She aims her arrow threateningly at Merlin. Suddenly she lets arrow and bow drop, and looks with rapture into his eyes.)

How mild your smile! That smile is my delight!
'Tis the first sunbeam breaking through the night!
In it I trust.

Merlin.

How beautifully wild!

Vivien.

Beam once again on me, oh radiance mild!
I saw it once before and did not fear.

Merlin.

When?

Vivien.

Know you not? And yet I was so near!
I saw you once amid a mighty crowd;
They marked you, and they called your name aloud,
Your glorious locks I saw in splendor streaming,
And in your eyes a gentle radiance beaming.
To greet that sudden vision beautiful,
I ran, and did it homage worshipful;
But when on me I saw your glances gleaming
I stole away, as though undutiful;
Still, still I am confused. Gaze not on me!
Far down into my deepest soul you see!
stole into the woods; the moon shone clear,
And in my spring I saw your features clear:
You stood before me in a waking dream,
And I to kneel to you in tears did seem!

(She steps back and covers her face with her hands, struggling to overcome her emotion. She stands facing the flowering plants, and does not seem to be concerned in what follows.)

Merlin

(who has not taken his eyes off her; softly, with forced calmness.)

Your spring? Where is it?

Lancelot.

As Vivien's spring 'tis 'mong our people known
Know you her not? Her father, Roas, slain
In battle was, She fearless roams through his domain
The arrow her sceptre and darksome rocks her throne,
But near her home there is a forest spring;
It is her favorite place of lingering:
When sunset redness in the forest gleams
'Tis there that Vivien listens, sings, and dreams.

(At the last words Vivien turns violently toward Lancelot without, however, looking at Merlin.)

Vivien.

Yet weep I not—Untruth I've spoken—
I did not weep! He forced from out my breast
What I would never have confessed.
My bow and arrow in the oaken
Forest, whose quietude is only broken
By me, allow the deer no rest.
Hallalee! Hallalee!
Deer, you may
Run away,
Still you'll be my arrow's prey!
For I hasten to o'ertake you
Over hill and over lea;
And whatever pace you make,
Ne'er from Vivien can you flee!
Crackle branches, rustle bushes!

MERLIN.

Ich weiss es nicht mehr — blick' mich nicht so an!
Das aber weiss ich und ich sag' dir's Mann!
Blickst du noch einmal mir so kalt in's Auge —
So kalt — so hart — wende dich weg von mir!
Ich weiss nicht, was ich zu vollbringen tauge:
Mit diesem Pfeil —

(Mit hastigem Griffe reisst sie den Pfeil aus der Linken und richtet ihn drohend gegen Merlin; plötzlich lässt sie Pfeil und Bogen fallen und blickt ihm entzückt in's Auge.)

Nun lächelst du, wie mild du lächeln kannst!
Man sagt von dir, dass du mit Blicken bannst:
Ich glaub' es wohl —

Merlin.
Du holdes, wildes Kind!

Viviane.
Blick' noch einmal so milde, so gelind!
So war dein Blick, da ich zuerst dich sah.

Merlin.
Wann — ?

Viviane.
Sahst mich nicht? ich war dir doch so nah'!
Ich sah dich einst mit vielem Volke zieh'n:
Die Menge wies auf dich: das ist Merlin!
Dein Lockenhaar sah ich im Winde wehen —
Ich lief hinzu, dich nah, ganz nah zu sehen:
Da, — ach, ich weiss nicht, wie ich's sagen soll:
Da strahlt' dein Aug' so weich, so gnadenvoll!
Dann schlich ich fort, und wollte fast vergehen
Vor Weh, vor Wonne, die mich überquoll!
Still! Still! Ich rede wirr, blick' mich nicht an!
Was zwingst du mir's aus meiner Seele, Mann?
Ich schlich zum Wald, aufstieg des Mondes Helle,
Ich kniete hin, ich kniet' an meiner Quelle —
Gleich, wie ein Traumbild, standest du vor mir,
Und ich, — in Thränen kniete ich vor dir!

(Sie tritt zurück und bedeckt ihr Antlitz mit den Händen, während sie ihre heftige Bewegung mühsam zu bekämpfen sucht. So steht sie, mit dem Antlitz gegen das Gebüsch gewendet, und scheint an dem unmittelbar Folgenden keinen Antheil zu nehmen.)

Merlin
(der sie unverwandt betrachtet hat — leise und mit erzwungener Ruhe.)
An welcher Quelle?

Lancelot.
Viviane's Quelle hat sie das Volk genannt —
Kennst du das Weib? Roas', des Herzogs, Spross;
Der Vater fiel — einsam haust sie im Schloss,
Mit ihren Jungfrauen, kühn und bogengewandt.
Doch nah' dem Schloss ist eine Quell' im Wald,
Die ist des Mädchens liebster Aufenthalt:
Dort, wenn des Abends Roth den Wald umsäumt,
Dort sitzt sie, lauscht den Wellen, singt und träumt.

(Bei den letzten Worten wendet sich Viviane, ohne Merlin anzublicken, heftig zu Lancelot.

Viviane.
Doch wein' ich nicht — es ist erlogen!
Ich weinte nicht! er zwang mir aus der Brust,
Was ich nicht wollt', was ich nicht wusst'.
Nein! nein! ich fasste Pfeil und Bogen,
Dem Hirsch im Walde bin ich nachgeflogen!
Jagen! Jagen! kennst du die Lust!
Hallali! hallali!
Hirschlein fein,
Streck' die Bein',
Hurtig über Stock und Stein!
Und wir rennen, und wir spähen,
Berg' und Wälder flieh'n vorbei!
Hei, da muss das Leid vergehen,
Und der Busen athmet frei!
Aeste knarren, Felsen rollen,

MERLIN.

Bend beneath my feet ye rushes!
On I go resistlessly,
All my sadness
Changed to gladness—
I am laughing loud and free!

Merlin

(who has kept his eyes fastened on her with sudden uncontrollable rapture.)

How beauteous! How wondrous fair!
Has Heaven robbed itself of all its bliss
And stamped it on her image with a kiss?
(He steps rapidly back and covers his eyes as if frightened at his own words.)

Arthur, Gawain, Glendower and Chorus.

All hail to thee, thou beauteous guest,
Could thou but here among us rest!
We ne'er from us would let thee part!
Most fair among the fair thou art!

Merlin.

Thou rapturously beauteous guest,
How strange to me my soul's unrest,
What fears are 'wakening in my heart,
Most fair among the fair thou art!

Lancelot.

All hail to thee, thou beauteous guest!
May thou here end thy roving quest!
For thee with life itself we'd part,
Most fair among the fair thou art!

Modred.

Ha! see, thou wondrous, beauteous guest,
Most strangely hast Merlin oppressed;
Once thine, farewell his magic art!
Most fair among the fair thou art!

Vivien.

Oh could I here but end my quest,
And with his love be ever blest;
Alas, my beating, quivering heart!
Mine is poor foolish woman's part.

Arthur
(advancing.

Glory and fame to Merlin we bequeath;
With these fresh oaken leaves his brow we wreathe,
To honor him whom all his foemen dread;
Most beauteous woman, crown him in my stead!

Vivien

(joyously takes the wreath, approaches Merlin and motions to him to bow his head. He stands there wrapt in musings; she approaches and touches his hand.)

Merlin
(starting back.

Away! Forbidden powers reign;
Frightful fancies rise to shock me!
Hedious groaning, voices of pain,
Devil's minions laughing mock me!
Clanking chains, demoniac might!
I nothing see—most hideous night!
(As it awakening from a dream.
Hence, evil woman, what seekest here?
What comest thou my soul anear?
(He seizes his harp.
Who called you here with wildering song
To trouble my harp's clear music strong?
(He bends over his harp; composedly and mildly:
Oh thou who bring'st my soul increase
Of sorrow, give me once more peace,
Thou heritage holy of a mother blest,
Unto her son give peace and rest,
Hear my call, oh mother blest!
Oh harp, when in my hands I'm holding thee,
I feel a sweet tranquillity!
Resound, resound, both loud and free,
For to my heart, oh harp, I'm pressing thee!
(He grasps the strings; they emit no sound. Deep silence; he starts back in dismay; once more he grasps the strings; no sound. He regards the harp anxiously, and tries a third time to awaken its music; but his hand fails him. With trembling voice he begins his song:
All hail, oh day of victory!
(He tears angrily at the harp-strings; unbroken silence. He lets his harp fall and covers his head.
Oh mother! What a warning send you me!

Vivien
(approaches him with fear.
Merlin!

Merlin.

Thou still here! Hence with ye!
Evil lurks within your features!
By the devil this was planned.

MERLIN.

Und wir rennen und wir tollen,
Immerzu in Saus und Braus!
Und das Sehnen
Und die Thränen
Und die Quelle lach' ich aus!

Merlin
(der sie unablässig betrachtet hat, nun plötzlich, in jäh hervorbrechendem Entzücken.)

Wie schön, o Gott, wie schön du bist!
Hat sich der Himmel aller Huld beraubt
Und goss er Alles auf ein einzig Haupt?
(Er tritt rasch zurück und bedeckt seine Augen, wie über die eigenen Worte erschrocken.)

Artus, Gawein, Glendower, Chor.
(zusammen.

Sei uns gegrüsst, du holder Gast!
O halt' in uns'rer Mitte Rast! —
Wie voller Huld an Seel' und Leib!
Fürwahr, es ist das schönste Weib!

Merlin.
Wie fühlt sich doch mein Herz erfasst!
Es sinkt auf mich, wie schwere Last!
Welch Bangen fasst mir Seel' und Leib!
Bringst du mir Unheil, holdes Weib?

Lancelot.
Sei uns gegrüsst, du holder Gast
Hast aller Edlen Herz erfasst!
Wer wagt nicht gerne Seel' und Leib,
Bekränzt ihn je ein solches Weib?

Modred.
Ha, seht! Wie hat der schöne Gast
Des heil'gen Sehers Herz erfasst!
Du hast gesiegt, o holdes Weib,
Bald ist er dein mit Seel' und Leib!

Viviane.
O welch' ein Wahn hat mich erfasst!
Was sprach ich doch in wilder Hast!
Ein Schauer strömt mir durch den Leib,
Bin ein unselig, thöricht Weib!

Artus
(vortretend.

Dem hohen Manne voller Ruhm und Glanz,
Ihm weih' ich dankend diesen Eichenkranz —
Leih' Du ihm Werth, dem schlichten Ruhmespfand:
Du schönstes Weib, kränz' ihn mit eig'ner Hand!

Viviane
(nimmt mit inniger Freude den Kranz, nähert sich Merlin, und winkt ihm, das Haupt zu neigen; er steht starr in sich versunken da; sie tritt nahe zu ihm und berührt seine Hand.)

Merlin
(zurückfahrend.

Hinweg! Welch Dunkel bricht herein!
Schrecklich Gebild steiget empor:
Unheil hör' ich — Stimme der Pein,
Stimme des Hohns gellt mir im Ohr —
Kettengeklirr — o schreckliche Macht!
Ich sehe nichts mehr — welch' tiefe Nacht —
(Er wacht wie aus Träumen auf.

Fort, Weib des Unheils! was suchst du hier?
Was zwingst du so die Seele mir
(Er ergreift seine Harfe.

Wer rief dich her? — mit wildem Gesang
Was störtest du meiner Harfe Klang?
(Er beugt sich zur Harfe nieder; ruhig und mild:

O die du meine Seele labst,
Die du mir oft den Frieden gabst,
Der heiligen Mutter heilig Erbe du,
Komm, meine Harfe! Fried' und Ruh'
Töne meinem Herzen zu!
Wie ich dich halte in meinen Händen,
Da schläft der Sturm und ruht versöhnt!
O töne laut, wie du noch nie getönt. —
Mein Lied, mein Lied, ich will es enden!
(Er greift mächtig in die Harfe; kein Ton erklingt; tiefe Stille; er fährt erschrocken zurück und greift noch einmal; kein Ton. Er betrachtet die Harfe, will zum drittenmal greifen; die Hand versagt ihm — mit zitternder Stimme beginnt er sein Lied:

Heil dir — o Tag! o Siegestag . . .
(Er zerrt wüthend an den Saiten; lange lautlose Stille. Er lässt die Harfe fallen und verhüllt sein Haupt.

Weh'! — Mutter, welches Zeichen schickst du mir?

Viviane
(nähert sich ihm furchtsam.

Merlin! —

Merlin.
Du noch hier? Fort mit dir!
Unheil liegt in deinen Zügen!
Der Böse hat dich mir gesandt!

MERLIN.

Vivien.

Oh hark not to your evil teachers,
Receive the garland from my hand!

Arthur.

May heaven turn away all evil!
(Pause.
Oh Merlin, rise with joyous mien,
Let sorrow not this day be seen!
This wreath, the gift of all the land,
Receive it, kneeling, from the fairest hand.

Merlin.

From her?
(Vehemently to Vivien:
From you? No, never!

Vivien.

Yes, kneel before me, 'tis right
That you should kneel before my might!
Once lay I weeping at your feet,—
Kneel now to me, as it is meet!
How in my heart I feel wrath burn!
To conquer you will come my turn,
And you shall kneel long as you live
To me, nor will I freedom give.

Merlin.

Hence! Hence! I hate you, devil fair!

Vivien.

I too can hate, and now my hate you dare!
Come maidens! come! Where are my bow and arrows?
We follow soon the covert narrows—
Hallalee to the chase! I press on the quarry!
With wounds a thousand the deer I'll worry

Now, Merlin, fare thee well! This day so bright
Shall leave upon thy head its parting token;
This wreath that should have crowned thy tresses light,
Torn lies it at your feet, and broken!
(She tears the wreath in pieces and throws them at Merlin's feet, then quickly turns to go. Commotion.

Chorus.

Ha, woman base! What are you doing?

Arthur
(joyfully to Merlin.
This day shall bring you greater name;
From me receive the crown of fame!
(He takes his own wreath and crowns Merlin with it.

Lancelot. Chorus.

This day you'll greater glory see!
You'll wear the crown of victory!
Through you the foe was put to flight,
Hail, Merlin brave, hail to your might!
(The warriors resume their Chorus.
Shameless treason came to naught,
For the right was ours,
Over foe and traitor both
Triumphed Christian powers!
Hail, King Arthur! Victor, hail!
May you o'er all foes prevail!
(Vivien appears once more on the Rock to the left, bow and arrow in hand, and looks down upon the scene. Merlin is lost in thought. Arthur grasps his hand and motions him to enter the castle with him. Both turn toward the gate. Merlin and Vivien's eyes meet once more.—Curtain.)

MERLIN.

Viviane.

Fort mit den Zaubern, die dich trügen!
Empfange den Kranz von meiner Hand!

Artus.

Der Himmel mag das Böse wenden!
(Pause.
Sieh' auf, Merlin, mit heitrem Blick!
Trübe dir nicht des Tages Glück!
Den Kranz, den ich dir zuerkannt,
Knie hin! empfang ihn von der schönsten Hand!

Merlin.

Von ihr?
(Heftig zu Viviane:
Von dir? Nein, nimmermehr!

Viviane.

Ja, kniee hin! so ist es recht!
Knieen sollst du, wie ein Knecht!
Einst lag' ich weinend auf den Knieen,
Nun kniee du, mein Held Merlin!
Ha, wie's mir auf der Seele brennt!
Dass ich dich ewig bannen könnt'!
Dass du mir kniest, so lang du lebst,
Dass du dich nimmermehr erhebst!

Merlin.

Fort! fort! Ich hasse dich, Teufelin!

Viviane.

Ha! kannst du hassen, ich kann's auch, Merlin!
Jungfrauen, kommt! Wo ist mein Pfeil, mein Bogen?
Wohin ist uns der Hirsch entflogen?
Hallali! Ihm nach! Ich muss ihn erjagen,
Tausend Wunden will ich ihm schlagen!

Leb' wohl, Merlin! Und dieses Tages Glanz,
In diesem Zeichen sollst du ihn begrüssen:
Auf deinem Haupte sollt' er ruh'n, der Kranz —
Hier ist der Kranz: zu deinen Füssen!
(Sie zerreisst den Kranz und wirft ihn Merlin heftig vor die Füsse, dann wendet sie sich rasch zum Abgehen. Stürmische Bewegung.)

Chor.

Ha, Frevlerin! Was hast du gewagt?

Artus
(feierlich zu Merlin.

Der Tag bringt dir noch höheren Glanz:
Ich setze dir auf's Haupt den Kranz!
(Er nimmt seinen eigenen Kranz vom Haupte und setzt ihn Merlin auf.

Lancelot, Chor.

Der Tag, er beut dir höchsten Glanz,
Nimm hin des Helden Ruhmeskranz;
Durch dich ward uns der Sieg verlieh'n,
Heil, zauberstarker Held Merlin!
(Die Krieger nehmen ihre frühere Weise wieder auf.

Was uns Tücke zugedacht,
Wurde doch zu Schanden;
Und aus wundenreicher Schlacht
Ist der Sieg erstanden!
Heil dem König, Heil dem Heer!
Heil des Tages Glanz und Ehr'!
(Viviane erscheint noch einmal auf dem Felsen zur Linken. Pfeil und Bogen in der Hand, und blickt auf die Scene zurück. Merlin ganz in sich verloren. Artus ergreift seine Hand und winkt ihm, in's Schloss zu folgen. Beide wenden sich dem Hauptthor zu; Merlins und Viviane's Blicke treffen sich noch einmal Zugleich fällt der Vorhang.)

[Ende des ersten Aktes.]

SECOND ACT.

Merlin's Magic Garden.

(In the middle background, groups of high trees with spreading branches, between which the ocean glitters. To the left, high trees and a luxuriant growth of rose bushes. A grassy seat, the left side of which is partially hidden by foliage. In the left foreground a small, richly ornate temple, to which lead steps upon which flowers have been strewn. From the temple a grassy knoll rises gently toward the bank to about the middle of the stage. It is a sunny afternoon.)

FIRST SCENE.

(Modred, Bedivere and several knights come from the background. Modred and the knights in full armor, Bedivere disguised as a monk.'

Modred.

You know my plans: King Arthur goes to war,
Like an adventurer, in countries far;
And while the combat he is there beginning,
Here from his friends his land we will be winning.
You, faithful Bedivere, and ye knights so true,
Stand you by me?

Bedivere and *Knights*
(grasping their swords.
By this good, gleaming sword I'll stand by you!

Bedivere.

In darksome prison I should still be bound
Unless for flight devices you had found.

The Knights.
All will go well, to you we faithful are!

Modred.

To glory I will be your guiding star;
Arthur's great foe, the King of Saxony,
Has promised me his faithful aid to be.
Comes Arthur home to fight, my downfall hoping,
At once with two great foemen we'll be coping;
Now, will you share this enterprise with me?

Bedivere and *Knights.*

Long live King Modred! We'll your allies be!

Modred.

Here soon he'll meet his favorite, friendly knights,
He's sure to give me trouble when he fights.—
So, Bedivere, quickly up this narrow way,
The King approaches—within hailing stay!
(Exit Bedivere to the left. Fanfares.

SECOND SCENE.

(Enter Arthur, Gawain, Lancelot, with many knights and warriors.)

Arthur.

Before unto the field, brave men, we go,
Merlin shall consecrate us 'gainst the foe;

ZWEITE AKT.

Merlin's Zauber-Garten.

Im mittleren Hintergrunde hohe weitästige Baumgruppen, zwischen denen das nahe Meer schimmert. Rechts hohe Bäume und üppiges Rosengebüsch. Eine Rasenbank, die linke Seite ein wenig durch Laub verdeckt. Links im Vordergrunde ein kleiner, reichgeschmückter Tempel, zu dem mit Blumen überstreute Stufen hinanführen. An den Tempel grenzend, zieht sich quer nach dem Hintergrunde zu eine kleine rasenartige Anhöhe, bis gegen die Mitte der Bühne, langsam ansteigend. — Sonniger Nachmittag.

ERSTE SCENE.

(Modred, Bedwyr und mehrere Ritter kommen aus dem Hintergrunde. Modred und die Ritter in voller Rüstung; Bedwyr als Mönch verkleidet.

Modred.

So wisst Ihr Alles: Artus zieht in's Feld,
Nach Abenteuern fährt er durch die Welt,
Fern über'm Meer Sinnloses zu beginnen:
Wir aber wollen hier das Reich gewinnen.
Ihr, treuer Bedwyr, und Ihr, Ritter werth,
Steht Ihr zu mir?

Bedwyr, Ritter
(an die Schwerter schlagend.
Wir stehn zu dir, bei diesem guten Schwert!

Bedwyr.

Im Kerker läg' ich jetzt noch festgebannt,
Halft Ihr mir nicht zur Flucht; — hier meine Hand!

Die Ritter.

Es wird gelingen, ja, wir steh'n zu dir!

Modred.

Zu Sieg und Ehren führt euch mein Panier.
Der uns schon oft bedrängt' der grimme Feind:
Der Sachsenkönig ist mit mir vereint;
Kehrt Artus heim und will er mich bekriegen,
Der Doppelmacht muss er sogleich erliegen.
So nehmt Ihr denn an Kampf und Ehren Theil?

Bedwyr und Ritter.

Lang' lebe Modred! König Modred Heil!

Modred.

Hierher entbot er seine Zeltgesellen,
Zum Reichsverweser wird er mich bestellen.
Geht, Bedwyr, rasch, hier diesen schmalen Pfad —
Harrt auf mein Zeichen! — Fort! der König naht!
(Bedwyr ab nach der linken Seite. Trompetenstösse.

ZWEITE SCENE.

(Artus, Gawein, Lancelot mit vielen Rittern und Kriegern kommen.)

Artus

Ihr Treuen, eh' wir fort zum Kampfe zieh'n,

And from this beauteous temple's quietude,
With holy thoughts and sacred rites imbued,
He'll send us forth to glorious victory.
If he is with us, who can 'gainst us be?
To him to whom our conquering might we owe,
Give a last thankful greeting e'er we go.

Modred
(aside, frightened.
Merlin!

Lancelot
(approaching him.
You did not know you'd hither come?

Arthur
(continuing.
My nephew Modred will remain at home,
I leave the trust and safety of my land
In his most firm and often-tested hand.

Lancelot
(advances.
Hear me, my King! I vouch for what I say!
This Modred plans his country to betray;
Unknown to him his plotting I've come nigh;
I charge him now, to you, with treason high.

Knights
(in confusion.
What says he? What's the charge?

Some of Modred's Knights.
Keep still, forsooth!

Arthur.
A weighty charge!

Lancelot.
Each word I speak is truth!

Arthur
(bitterly.
Treason once more! Can it be true?
Unhappy country mine, I pity you!
With foes like floods around you surging
And threatening to sweep you o'er,
Is treachery too your downfall urging?
Must succumb you such foes before?

Lancelot.
I can't be silent: let me tell you—

Modred.
Be silent, slanderer, or I will fell you;
Call me not traitor to this land!

Lancelot.
Hark and give answer!

Modred.
No more will I stand!
(He draws his sword.
Thus speak I—Now for your base life take care.

Lancelot.
Let Heaven judge!—I dare it if you dare!
(Drawing his sword.

Arthur
(stepping between them.
Not so, sir knights! Judgment to Merlin leave!
Far more than swords, far more than words of men,
More than the stars in heaven I'd him believe!
Deep down into each heart he sinks his ken!
Stand you near him, he will the truth discover.
His word, his look will all that's false uncover.

THIRD SCENE.

Merlin
(descends from the knoll.
King Arthur!

MERLIN.

Rief ich euch her zum Tempel des Merlin.
Von dieser Stätte seliger Einsamkeit,
Nur frommer Andacht, heiligem Thun geweiht,
Schickt er in fernstes Land den Scherblick,
Führt in der Ferne uns zu Sieg und Glück.
Der überall uns schützt mit seiner Macht,
Ihm sei der letzte Abschiedsgruss gebracht!

Merlin!

Modred
(erschrocken bei Seite.

Lancelot
(an ihn herantretend.
Du bebst? — Hast du die Stätte nicht gekannt?

Artus
(fortfahrend.
Mein Neffe Modred bleibe hier im Land.
Schon oft erprobt' es seinen kühnen Muth,
Dem Klugen, Treuen geb' ich's in die Hut.

Lancelot
(tritt vor.
Hör' mich, mein König! Ritter, hört mich an!
Des Reiches Hut vertraust du diesem Mann.
Schon lange acht' ich sorgsam seines Pfads:
Der Arglist zeih' ich ihn, des Hochverraths!

Ritter
(durcheinander.
Was sagt er? welch ein Wort?!

Einige der Ritter Modreds.
Schweig, frecher Mund!

Artus.
Mann, welch ein Wort!

Lancelot.
Ein Wort mit gutem Grund!

Artus
(in tiefstem Schmerze aufklagend.
Verrath? Noch einmal? Wär' es wahr?
Mein armes Volk, umrungen von Gefahr,
Von Völkerfluthen rings umstritten,
Von tausend Feinden hart bedroht,
Wühlt noch Verrath in deiner Mitten,
Es ist dein Untergang — es ist mein Tod!

Lancelot.
Nicht schweigen darf ich: lass' dir melden —

Modred.
Mein König, lässest du vor allen Helden
Mit solchem Lügenwort mich schmäh'n?

Lancelot.
Hör' und erwidre!

Modred.
Ich dir Rede steh'n?
(Er zieht sein Schwert.
So red' ich — so beweise, was du klagst!

Lancelot
(sein Schwert ziehend.
Ein Gotteskampf! — Ich wag's, wenn du es wagst!

Artus
(zwischen sie tretend.
Nicht so, Ihr Ritter! Seht, dort kommt Merlin!
Mehr als auf Schwerter und auf Menschenmund,
Mehr, als auf Sterne, baue ich auf ihn:
Er blickt hinab in jedes Herzens Grund.
Tritt du vor ihn, er wird die Wahrheit nennen:
Sein Wort, — sein Blick, er zwingt dich zu bekennen!

DRITTE SCENE.

VORIGE. MERLIN.

Merlin
(war auf der Anhöhe erschienen und kommt jetzt herab.
Mein König! —

Arthur.
Hail, noble seer!

Merlin.
Who there fights?

Arthur.
Step nearer, Modred!

Modred
(in anger.
Have I lost all rights?
I vindicate them in this public place?

Lancelot.
You are afraid!

Modred.
No! 'Tis a slander base!
No—spite the magic of the seer
You lie!

Arthur.
It is my wish! step near!

Modred
(facing Merlin.
Here stand I: speak—examine—weigh me!

Lancelot.
Of treason high accused by me he stands!
His angry looks do not dismay me.
O Merlin! save these threatened lands.

Merlin
(after a pause, calmly.
Clear is your look. No treason there is stored—
But should it hidden be deep in your heart,
I summon, in the name of our high Lord,
It from its secret hiding place to start!

Modred.
No trait'rous thoughts have I to rue:
To King and country I am true!

Merlin
(after regarding him awhile.
In him I find no trace of sin.

Lancelot.
No sin!

Several Knights.
Hail, Modred! Hail! From crime you cleared have been!

Lancelot.
Is't possible? Yet never wrong was he!

Arthur.
Praise God! For peace thou'st given back to me!
(To the knights.
And now to ship, to see new victories!
Those who like beasts around our coast are roaring,
In their own lands I'll seek those enemies.
Merlin, farewell! Think oft of me while warring!
(Embraces him.

The Knights.
Merlin, farewell! Think oft of us while warring!

Merlin.
Farewell, my King! Well I'll remember thee;
To serve our cause no hand could firmer be;
You are our strength, you are our fortune's hope;
No one so bravely with our foes can cope!
Fare ye all well!

The Knights.
(brandishing their swords.
Now on to victories!
To battle glad we go!
Those who like beasts around our coast are roaring,
In their own land we seek the enemies.
Now on to victories!
To battle glad we go!
(Exeunt all but Merlin.

MERLIN.

Artus.
Gruss dir, Edler!

Merlin.
Welcher Streit?

Artus.
Tritt näher, Modred!

Modred
(wüthend.
Schmach und bittres Leid!
Ich Rede stehen vor dem ganzen Heer?

Lancelot.
Du weigerst dich?

Modred.
Nein, Lästrer, nimmermehr!
Trotz Höllenkunst und Sehertrug:
Du lügst!

Artus.
Tritt hin! Es ist genug!

Modred
(vor Merlin tretend.
Hier bin ich: rede — prüfe — frage!

Lancelot.
Des Hochverrathes hab' ich ihn gezieh'n:
Du, Seher, richte über meine Klage!
Nicht Lügen kann er vor Merlin.

Merlin
(nach einer Pause ruhig.
Dein Blick ist rein, als wie der reinste Stern —
Doch bärg' die Schuld sich auch im tiefsten Grund:
Im Namen Gottes ruf' ich ihr, des Herrn.
Herauf und rede durch des Sünders Mund!

Modred.
Ich red' und rufe sonder Scheu:
Dem König dien' ich wahr und treu!

Merlin
(nachdem er ihn eine Weile betrachtet.
Ich finde keine Schuld an ihm.

Lancelot.
Merlin!

Mehrere Ritter.
Heil, Modred, Heil! Die Klage fällt dahin!

Lancelot.
Wär's möglich? Niemals trog des Sehers Blick!

Artus.
Dank dir! Den Frieden gabst du mir zurück!
(zu den Rittern:
Nun fort, zur See! Zu neuem Siegeslauf!
Die unsre Küste ungezähmt bedräuen:
Im eignen Land such' ich die Feinde auf! —
Leb wohl, Merlin! Gedenke mein in Treuen!
(Er umarmt ihn herzlich.

Die Ritter.
Lebt wohl, Merlin, gedenkt an uns in Treuen!

Merlin.
Leb' wohl, mein Fürst! In Treuen denk' ich dein;
Der Briten Ruhm, er ruht auf dir allein;
Du, unsre Kraft, du, unsres Glückes Pfand,
Kehr' bald zurück ins theure Heimathland! —
Lebt Alle wohl!

Die Ritter
(die Schwerter schwingend.
Wohlauf zum Siegeslauf,
Zu frohem Kampf wohlauf!
Die unsre Küste ungezähmt bedräuen,
Im eignen Lande suchen wir sie auf!
Wohlauf zum Siegeslauf,
Zu frohem Kampfe wohlauf!
(Alle ausser Merlin ab.)

FOURTH SCENE.

Merlin

(looks after them and motions farewell to them; he descends, faces the temple and goes up several steps; he turns back and for some time gazes in silence upon the temple.

Oh sacred site! Oh holy place of rest!
With heavy heart to you I come;
What leads me to this peaceful, restful home?
It is the search for your quiescence blest.
Must I from here in sorrow further roam?
Could I but rest like you so calm and mild,
Could I but rest!—Alas, from here I'm driven,
And shall I ne'er know rest and peace?
Ne'er find this sorrow's blest surcease?
O'er hill, o'er meadow, in forest so wild,
O'er mountains sought I in headlong flight
To soothe my senses' fearful affright;
And yet I am not of my guilty thoughts shriven.
In deepest night, in chamber darkened,
Vainly for comforting voices I've hearkened,
Hoping 'gainst hope to be forgiven—
And yet I am not of my guilty thoughts shriven:
O image sweet!

(Exeunt dreamily.

FIFTH SCENE

DEMON, THEN VIVIEN

Demon

(appears from the right.

She comes—she's wandering in sorrow brooding,
She's hither drawn by secret evil powers.
Fair huntress wild, we soon will count you ours!
To do the devil's will you I am goading;
Oh spirits mine! into your realm she's coming,
Now weave your artful magic fast around her,
Your amorously quivering lay be humming,
And to the seer's perdition now confound her.

Vivien.

(enters from the right.

Where am I? Again I've wandered astray!
How can I return? Who'll show me the way?

Demon.

Hail, noble virgin!

Vivien.

Who calls so near?

(She steps nearer.

Demon.

Most beautiful goddess, dwellest thou here?

Vivien.

Why, What mean you?

Demon.

To Goddesses I've spoken
Right here, naught can surprise; so near hell's portals
Each flower, each leaf is here a ghostly token;
Here all about us dwell the fair immortals.
A weary wand'rer entered I this grove
Where magic is with nature interwove,
And, as I listen, from this hall I seem
To hear the the music of a rapturous dream,
But no one answers though I stand and call;
What may be hidden in this hall?

Vivien.

I will go in.
(They seek in vain to open the portals.

Demon.

In vain is all our trouble,
'Tis as I thought—now let us wander on!

VIERTE SCENE.

Merlin

(sieht und winkt ihnen nach; dann kommt er herab, tritt vor den Tempel, besteigt einige Stufen, als wollte er eintreten; dann kommt er zurück und betrachtet ihn stillschweigend eine geraume Weile.

Mein Heiligthum! O Stätte sel'ger Ruh' —
Mit meinem Herzen bang und schwer,
Was treibt mich heut' in deine Stille her?
Ach, dir — ach deinem Frieden drängt mich's zu,
Allein mein Friede wohnt in dir nicht mehr!
Wer ruhen könnt', wie du, so still, so mild!
Wer ruhen könnt'! — Mich aber treibt's von dannen.
Ach, nirgends, nirgends Ruh und Rast!
Hier auf dem Herzen diese Last!
In Thal und Auen, in Wald und Gefild,
Auf allen Bergen in wilder Flucht,
Hab' ich des Herzens Frieden gesucht!
Ich kann dich nicht lassen, ich kann dich nicht bannen,
In tiefer Nacht in stiller Kammer
Vergebens kämpf' ich in bitterstem Jammer,
Wollte mich wappnen, mich ermannen —
Ich kann dich nicht lassen, kann dich nicht bannen:
Du süsses Bild!

(Sinnend und träumend links ab.

FUENFTE SCENE.

Dämon, dann Viviane.

Daemon

(erscheint von rechts.

Sie kommt — sie irrt umher in dumpfem Sinnen,
Es zieht sie fort mit heimlichen Gewalten —
Nun, Jägerin, nun gilt's, dich festzuhalten,
Die schönste Beute sollst du mir gewinnen!
O Geisterreich, sie tritt in deine Mitte,
Mit süssem Zauber sollst du sie umwehen,
Umwinden eng und enger ihre Schritte,
Dass Beide straucheln und zu Grunde gehen.

Viviane

(kommt von rechts.

Wo bin ich? Verfehlt' ich wieder den Pfad?
Wie komm' ich nun heim? Wen bitt' ich um Rath?

Daemon.

Heil, edle Jungfrau!

Viviane.

Da ruft es ja!

(sie tritt näher.

Daemon.

O holdeste Göttin, hausest du da?

Viviane.

Versteh' dich nicht.

Daemon.

Göttinnen hier zu finden,
Beim Thor der Hölle! nicht soll's mich erstaunen:
Gespenstisch wallt es rings in Thal und Gründen,
Aus Quell und Wipfel hört' ich's seltsam raunen;
Ein milder Wanderer trat ich in den Hain —
Fürwahr die Stätte muss verzaubert sein.
Denn, als ich kam: da — aus der Halle drang
Ein wundersamer klagender Gesang;
Doch öffnet Niemand, wie ich ruf' und frag' —
Was wohl die Halle bergen mag?

Viviane.

Ich will hinein.

(Sie suchen vergebens das Thor zu öffnen.

Daemon.

Die Mühe ist verloren.
Ich ahn' es wohl — ei, lass uns weitergeh'n!

Yet stay—both lock and bolt seem to be
  gone:
This temple surely is some magic bubble.
I've wandered much, seen much, and
  much I've known
Of magic powers around the devil's
  throne;
In beauteous temples he conceals the
  power
Of magic treasures till an evil hour;
Nor lock nor bolt doth guard the regal
  portal,
And yet no one through it can reach the
  hall;
It opens not to any one who's mortal,
But only at the devil's mighty call.

Vivien.

I must go in!

Demon
                                (laughing.
Against it press outright!
For beauty will o'ercome the master's
  might.
Now fare thee well. No longer may I
  tarry;
The sun is sinking in the Western sea—

Vivien.

Oh could some power me through this
  portal carry!

Demon.

Farewell!

Vivien.

O lovely portal, ope to me!
                    (The portal flies open.

Demon.

See an altar!

Vivien

And a veil—there, higher!

Demon.

Around it suffusing are roseate fire!
Enter! You will not, dare not go?
          (He enters and hands her the veil.

Vivien.
                        (holding the veil.
How airy and soft!
(She playfully throws it above her, where it remains suspended and glows.
              O rapturous glow!

Demon.

Hark! Hark! Those sounds!

Vivien.

Know you what power there lurks?

Demon.

Not I.

Vivien
                      (suddenly trembling.
And if it harm e'er works?

Chorus of Spirits
                                (unseen.
We're coming from petals, from trees
  and from mountains,
From nebulous cloud-forms and glittering fountains;
We're coming, obeying the call of our
  Lord,
Most beautiful goddess, by us be adored!
                            (Exit Demon.

BALLET.

A spring suddenly flows from among the bushes; rosy clouds float in from all sides. The bushes part. From the fountain rise water-sprites in green glittering veils. From the clouds float down winged air-sprites in flowing white drapery. Out of the rocks and earth come the earth-sprites with golden ornaments. From the bushes issue the flower-sprites, representing various flowers. Toward the close is seen distantly on the ocean, in a shell drawn by dolphins, the queen of the mermaids, surrounded by her subjects.—Enter Merlin.

SIXTH SCENE.

VIVIEN. MERLIN.

Vivien

(sees Merlin and starts back with a half-smothered cry. The spirits vanish. The veil falls over a bush in the foreground.)

Sieh doch, nicht Schloss noch Riegel ist
zu seh'n:
Die Halle ist mit ihrem Herrn ver-
schworen.
Viel wandert' ich, sah Vieles nah' und
fern,
Von Zaub'rern hört' ich, mächt'gen Gei-
sterherrn.
In heiligen Hallen birgt sich ihre Macht,
Der Zauberschätze wunderreiche Pracht.
Nicht Schloss noch Riegel schliesset
ihre Pforte,
Doch ist gesorgt, dass uns kein Müh'n
gelingt:
Das Thor erschliesst sich nur des Mei-
sters Worte,
Und dem nur, der den Meister selber
zwingt.

Viviane.

Ich muss hinein!

Daemon
(lachend.

Versuch es immerhin!
Die Schönheit ist der Meister Meisterin!
Nun lebe wohl, nicht länger darf ich
säumen,
Nach Westen lenkt die Sonne ihren
Lauf. —

Viviane.

Ach, einmal nur in diesen Zauber-
räumen!

Daemon.

Leb' wohl!

Viviane.

O liebe Pforte, thu' dich auf!
(Das Thor springt auf.

Daemon.

Ha, ein Altar!

Viviane.

Und drüber — ein Schleier! —

Daemon.

Und rings ergiesst sich ein rosiges
Feuer!
Tritt ein! du willst nicht? wagst es
nicht?
(Er tritt hinein und bringt den Schleier heraus.

Viviane.
(den Schleier fassend.

Wie duftig, wie weich!
(Sie wirft ihn spielend empor, er bleibt schwe-
bend oben, er leuchtet.

O wonniges Licht!

Daemon.

Horch, horch! es tönt!

Viviane.

Kennst du des Zaubers Kraft?

Daemon.

Ich nicht.

Viviane
(plötzlich erschauernd.

Und ob's nicht Unheil schafft?

Geisterchor
(unsichtbar.

Wir kommen aus Kelchen und Kronen
und Klüften,
Aus glitzernden Wellen, aus säuselnden
Lüften,
Wir kommen, wir folgen dem mächtigen
Herrn,
Der Holden, der Holden, wir dienen ihr
gern!
(Dämon ab.

(Eine Quelle schiesst plötzlich zwischen dem
Gebüsch hervor, rosige Wolken erheben sich von
allen Seiten; die Büsche theilen sich auseinander.
Aus den Quellen steigen Wassergeister empor,
in grünen Schleiern, glitzernden Gewändern. Aus
den Wolken herab schweben Luftgeister, ge-
flügelt, in weissen wallenden Schleiern. Aus den
Felsen und der Erde erscheinen Erdgeister, mit
goldenem Geschmeide behängt, aus den Gebüschen Blumengeister, in bunter Gewandung man-
nigfache Blumen darstellend. Am Schlusse, in
der Ferne auf der Meeresfläche sichtbar, in einer
Muschel, von Delphinen gezogen, die Königin
der Meerfrauen, von ihren Schaaren umschwom-
men. — Geisterreigen. — Merlin kommt.)

SECHSTE SCENE.

VIVIANE. MERLIN.

Viviane
(erblickt Merlin und fährt mit einem halbunter-
drückten Schrei zurück. Geister verschwinden.
Der Schleier fällt auf ein Gebüsch nahe im
Vordergrunde.

MERLIN.

Merln.

Thou! Thou! What wilt—what seek'st thou here?

Vivien
(quickly restraining herself.)

Not thee, for whom I've shed many a tear;
From my maiden throng I have gone astray—
A boy did counsel me, I lost the way!
Canst thou the way unto my castle show?

Merlin.

Thither's the way!

Vivien.

By yon flowery row?

Merlin.

By yonder row.

Vivien.

Now fare thee well!

Merlin.

Farewell!
(He sees the veil.)
The veil that wrought this wrong to me!

Vivien.

To thee?—Forgive, I knew it not—to thee?

Merlin.

And there—the portal! Whose traitor hand——?

Vivien.

It oped itself at my command.

Merlin.

It oped for thee—for thee? O eternal might!

Vivien.

Forgive! I did not know it was not right!
The veil I take and high I fling—

When, lo, dancing spirits about me sing.
'Tis rapturous!

Merlin.

You have touched the veil?
O horror!

Vivien.

Wherein did I thus fail?
So airy 'tis and so soft!
(She endeavors to take it again.)

Merlin.
(holding her back.)
Hold on! Hold on!

Vivien.

'Twere lovely if o'er my locks it were thrown!

Merlin.

Child, child! kneel low, give thanks to the power
That watched over you in an evil hour!
The treacherous veil once in your hand,
You are mistress made of the spirit band.
But should its magic you once enfold,
You, mortal one, would suffer terrors untold!
Should I once throw it your fair form over,
Or with it only your ringlets cover,
Woe! Woe!
The lovely rose-bushes would sink out of sight,
Around you tower rocks black as night,—
Here, lost to all you cherish, you would lie;
The curse would lighten only when you die;
And did you even sway the highest rule,
Your power would be the plaything of the ghoul,
And you the slave of him you could not flee;
And even my power could never set you free!

Vivien.

Most fearful tale! I feel such dread!

Merlin.
Du? du? Was willst du, was suchst du hier?

Viviane
(sich rasch fassend.
Fürwahr nicht dich! Wir tollten im Revier,
Von meinen Jungfrau'n hab' ich mich verirrt,
Ein Knabe wies mich her, — der dumme Hirt!
Ich wollt' in's Schloss, weisst du den Weg?

Merlin.
Dort ist der Weg?

Viviane.
Dort am Gartengeheg?

Merlin.
Dort am Geheg.

Viviane.
Hab Dank, leb' wohl.

Merlin.
Leb' wohl.
(Er erblickt den Schleier.
Der Schleier? ha! Wer drang so kühn zu mir?

Viviane.
Zu dir? — Vergieb, ich wusst' es nicht — zu dir?!

Merlin.
Und dort — die Pforte! Wessen Verrath —?

Viviane.
Sie that sich auf, als ich sie bat.

Merlin.
Sie that sich auf — vor dir? O ewige Macht!

Viviane.
Vergieb! es war thöricht, war unbedacht!
Den Schleier nahm ich und warf ihn empor,
Sieh', da umschloss mich ein tanzender Chor.
Gar herrlich war's!

Merlin.
Du fasstest ihn an,
Den Schleier?

Viviane.
Ja, was läg' wohl daran?
So duftig ist er, so zart!
(Sie will den Schleier ergreifen.

Merlin
(sie zurückhaltend.
Halt ein!

Viviane.
Ich hüllte mir gern die Locken darein...

Merlin.
Kind, Kind! knie' hin und danke der Macht,
Die heute dich gütig schützend bewacht!
Der tückische Flor in deiner Hand,
Er hat dir die seligen Geister gebannt: —
Doch fasste dich selbst sein Zauber an:
Dich Sterbliche träf' er mit schrecklichstem Bann!
Wenn ich den Schleier um's Haupt dir führte,
Wenn er dir nur die Locken berührte:
Weh dir!
Die holden Gebüsche versänken um dich,
Felsen umschlössen dich fürchterlich,
Hier lägst du fest, unrettbar festgebannt. —
Der Tod nur löst den Bann, der dich umwand:
Und herrschtest du auf höchstem Geisterthron:
Du wärest machtlos, aller Geister Hohn,
Im Zauber lägst du, könntest nie entflieh'n —
Wärst du auch stark gewesen, wie Merlin!

Viviane.
Ha, grausenvoll! mir wird so bang!

Merlin.

Be not afraid! Look up, again be cheerful!
For Heaven's favor watches o'er you!

Vivien
(starting.
Where am I? What did I? Speak you true?
(Brief pause—then quietly:
Forgive! Farewell!

Merlin
(lost in gazing upon her.
My Vivien!

Vivien
(laughing wildly.
Woe to be held by you in bondage fearful!
And yet the bonds were almost wrought by me!—
Woe, woe is me!
(In sudden grief:
No, nevermore, by you!
Farewell!
(Turns to go.

Merlin.
My Vivien!

Vivien
(stamps her foot in anger.
Must I be pitied in my pain!
(Bursts into tears and covers her face with her hands.

Merlin.
You tremble and weep—O look on me!

Vivien.
Farewell! Farewell!

Merlin.
Oh must you go?
(Takes her hand.
Oh let me to my loving bosom press you!
And let my love's swift passion bless you!

Vivien.
Oh mock me not in bitter pain!

Merlin.
My loved one!

Vivien
(tearing herself away.
You pity me! Your pity I'll not have!
Because I weep you think I pity crave!
Your pity spare, I'll not remain!
There lurked no sorrow in my mien—
But tears of sorrow you have seen!

Merlin.
Are you then angry?

Vivien.
That I could not be.
I am a fool—the old wound burns anew!
Woe's me! My heart's deep pain you see—
Rejected, repulsed by you—by you!

Merlin.
Oh loved one, let me be forgiven,
See, at your feet, I'm kneeling even!

Vivien.
You hated me—you hated me—
And from your own lips I had to hear it!
Way with your magic might—I fear it!
Oh Lord of Heaven, pray pity me!
(She rapidly turns to go.

Merlin.
Remain with me! Beloved wife!

Vivien
(remains as though startled.
Beloved wife!
'Twas thus—you called—Oh beloved wife!

Merlin
(approaching her with open arms.
My Vivien!

Merlin.
O sei nicht bang! Blick auf, du bist gerettet!
Des Himmels Huld schwebt segnend über dir!

Viviane
(auffahrend.
Wo bin ich? was that ich? wehe mir!
(kurze Pause, dann ruhig.
Vergieb' — leb' wohl —

Merlin
(in ihren Anblick versunken.
Viviane! — — —

Viviane
(plötzlich auflachend.
Ha, ha, wie toll! an dich, an dich gekettet:
Zu dir gebannt! Bald hätt' ich's selbst gethan!
Zu dir gebannt!
(plötzlich aufklagend.
Nein, nimmermehr zu dir!
Leb' wohl!
(will gehen

Merlin.
Viviane! —

Viviane
(bleibt stehen und stampft voll Zorn.
Soll ich vergeh'n in dieser Pein!
(Sie bricht in Thränen aus und bedeckt ihr Antlitz mit den Händen.

Merlin.
Du zitterst, du weinst — o sieh' mich an!

Viviane.
Leb' wohl, leb' wohl —

Merlin.
O willst du geh'n?
(Er nimmt ihre Hand.
O lass dein Haupt an meine Schulter lehnen!
Wie schön du bist in deinen Thränen!

Viviane.
Weidest du dich an meinem Schmerz?

Merlin.
Du Holde!

Viviane
(ihre Hand losreissend.
O wohl, dich dauert's, du gnädiger Mann,
Dass ich die Thränen nicht halten kann!
Spare dein Mitleid, schone dein Herz!
Es war nicht Schmerz, wie du gemeint —
Es war nur Zorn, wenn ich geweint!

Merlin.
Zürnst du mir noch?

Viviane.
Was wär' da Zornes werth?!
Ich Thörin! entbrennt's denn ewig neu in mir?
Weh, wie sich mein Herz in Grimm verzehrt —
Verworfen, geschmäht von dir, — von dir!

Merlin.
So zürnst du noch? o lass mich's büssen,
Holde, Süsse, zu deinen Füssen . . . .

Viviane.
Du hassest mich, du hassest mich:
Aus deinem Munde muss ich's hören!
Fort! Fort! Es will mir die Sinne zerstören —
O Herr des Himmels, erbarme dich!
(Sie will rasch abgehen

Merlin.
O bleibe hier! Geliebtes Weib!

Viviane
(erschrocken stehen bleibend.
Geliebtes Weib —
Du warst's — du riefst — du riefst mich so an?

Merlin
(mit offenen Armen auf sie zugehend.
Viviane!

MERLIN.

Vivien
(falling around his neck.
O beloved man!
Is't true? Is't true? Or is it a dream?

Merlin.
Let upon me your fond eyes beam!
My Vivien for you I yearn!
And did I then hate you? And did I spurn
The breast 'gainst which my heart is beating,
You who are all my hope and longing,
Whose features in passionate visions thronging
I've seen since I repelled your greeting!

Vivien
(in rapture.
In passion's rapture, love, I hold you!
My Merlin, how brave, how noble you are!
Hark! while unto my breast I fold you,
The forest voices echo far
My heart's enraptured, joyous beating;
I quiver like flower, and grass and grove;
Such is the first impassioned greeting
Of wakening love to wakening love!
The world is cold, and drear and sad—
Within your heart my love I feel!
With trembling, quivering passion glad,
I cling to you for woe or weal!

Merlin
(with growing passion
Did I, my love, once shun you? Forgive!
You dazzled me like the summer sun;
I stood confused, but now I've won
The love that makes it joy to live.
And cannot I, by dear Love shriven,
Live and love on by you forgiven?
Oh let me now to my bosom fold you—
Do you not hear my heart swiftly beating?
Let me more closely press and hold you!
'Tis passion fierce its fierce mate meeting;
Our hearts are toward each other flooding,
And love within our hearts is budding,
As flood the rivers toward the sea,
As bloom the flowers on the lea.
O lordly day! O happy meeting!
To-day, to-day I've won love's greeting!

Merlin and *Vivien.*
Love's shining light is thrown around us,
I feel his warm caressing form;
I know full well now that he's found us,
He'll keep us safely from all harm.
(Stormy embrace.
(Merlin and Vivien seat themselves down upon the grassy seat in the foreground. Twilight. Rocks and trees radiant in the increasing glow of the setting sun.

Merlin.
My heart is kindling, inly-warm!
O lean your beauty on my arm!
How closely to your form you've bound me,
Your waving tresses flood around me!
You shudder—I feel your quivering form,
Trembling in passion's resistless storm!
(He kisses her long and lovingly.

Vivien.
The storm is past and you, caressing,
Hold me in your embrace so warm!
Yet fear I!—Loved one,—is it harm?
Yes, it is true. Your lips on mine are pressing!
Yes, it is true, and yet it seems
The memory fond of blissful dreams!

Vivien.
The storm is past and you, caressing,
Hold me in your embrace so warm!
You are the calm after the storm—
Your lips against my lips are pressing!
Oh stay with me, oh do not wander
Hence to the cruel, fearful wars.
Oh linger on these blissful shores!
Oh stay with me, oh do not ever wander—
Tell me that you will never leave me lone!
Fast as the heaven holds its bright stars yonder
Will I hold you, beloved, all my own!

Merlin.
The storm is past, and you, caressing,
I'll hold in my embrace so warm!
You are the calm after the storm;
Your lips against my lips are pressing!
I'll stay with you, I will not wander

MERLIN.

Viviane
(fällt ihm um den Hals.
Heissgeliebter Mann!
Ist's wahr? ist's wahr? O kann es denn
 sein?

Merlin.
Ich liebe Dich! Sieh', ich bin Dein!
Nicht länger trag' ich diese Last!
Dich hätt' ich verworfen, o Dich gehasst?
Dich, der mein Herz entgegenbebt,
Dich, meine Sehnsucht, mein Verlangen!
Mein tägliches Sinnen, mein nächtliches
 Bangen,
Das Liebste, das mir auf Erden lebt!

Viviane
(aufjauchzend.
Könnt' ich die ganze Welt umschlingen!
Geliebter, wie hold, wie herrlich du
 bist!
O alle Räume sollten klingen
Vom Glück, das mir erschienen ist!
Dich wollt' ich lassen! Dich vergessen,
In blutiger Jagd, durch Wald und Haid'!
Ach, unbezwingbar, unermessen
Wuchs meine Liebe und mein Leid!
Bang ist's und fremde in der Welt,
Daheim ist's nur bei Dir, bei Dir!
O Wonne, die mich umfangen hält!
Unendliche Seligkeit zittert in mir!

Merlin
(in immer steigender Wärme.
Hab' ich Dir Herbes gesagt? Vergieb!
So blendend erscheinst Du meinem Blick,
Ich stand verzagt vor meinem Glück!
Nun aber, komm, Du holdes Lieb,
Nimm, mich zur Busse ganz dahin,
Nimm, was ich hab' und was ich bin!
An meinem Herzen will ich Dich hegen,
Fühlst Du die Sehnsucht, die es ver-
 zehrt?
O fühlst Du, fühlst Du an seinen Schlä-
 gen,
Wie es an Dir zu sterben begehrt?
Ja, Süsse, lass uns vergehen zusammen,
Lass uns in einer Gluth erflammen —
Ein Liebesjauchzen: ich bin Dein! —
Ich liebe Dich! Sei mein! sei mein!

Merlin und Viviane.
O Tag! o herrlichste der Sonnen!
Mein Liebstes hab' ich mir gewonnen!

Es kam das Glück aus lichten Höhen,
Und mich umschmiegt's so süss, so
 warm;
Ich weiss, es wird nicht von mir gehen,
Ich halt es ja in meinem Arm!
(Stürmische Umarmung.
(Merlin und Viviane haben sich auf der Rasen-
 bank rechts im Vordergrunde niedergelassen.
 Abenddämmerung. Felsen und Bäume von
 immer hellerem Roth überflossen.

Merlin.
Mein Herz erglüht so innig-warm,
O schmiege Dich in meinen Arm,
So, fest und fester umschliesse mich,
Mit Deinen Locken umfliesse mich,
Du schauerst — es zittert Dein süsser
 Leib,
Wie schön Du bist, Du zitterndes Weib!
(Er küsst sie lang und innig.

Viviane.
Das ist der Sehnsucht stille Stunde,
Da ich am Quell nach Dir verlangt! —
O lass mich! — Liebster — lass — mir
 bangt,
So ist es wahr, Dein Mund an meinem
 Munde —
So ist es wahr, ich fass' es kaum;
Erfüllt, erfüllt mein wonniger Traum!

Viviane.
Das ist der Sehnsucht stille Stunde,
So ist's erfüllt! so hab' ich's erlangt!
O Du, nach dem ich still gebangt —
So halt ich Dich im trauten Bunde!
O bleibe mein! Ach, in die Ferne,
Zu lauten Manneskämpfen hin,
Zieht Dich Dein hoher Heldensinn!
O bleibe mein! Auch in der fernsten
 Ferne!
Sag' mir, dass nie dein Lieben mich ver-
 lässt —
Ach, wie der Himmel festhält seine
 Sterne,
So hielt ich gern Dich, o Geliebter, fest!

Merlin.
Das ist der Sehnsucht stille Stunde!
O Du, nach der ich heiss verlangt,
O Du, nach der ich still gebangt,
So halt ich Dich an meinem Munde;
Ich bleibe Dein! In öde Ferne,

Hence to the fearful, cruel wars;
I'll linger on these blissful shores!
I'll stay with you, oh never will I wander,
And never, never, will I leave you lone!
Fast as the heaven holds its bright stars yonder,
Will I hold you, beloved, all my own!

(The sun sets; Merlin and Vivien sit in calm embrace, gazing into each others eyes. Tumultuous noise behind the scene).

Voices
(behind the scenes.
Merlin! Merlin!

(The tumult increases. Night comes on. The moon, at moments brightly shining, at times behind the clouds).

Merlin.

What means that noise? Who calls me?

Glendower
(behind the scene.
Protect me now, Merlin!

SEVENTH SCENE.

(Glendower and several warriors enter hastily; immediately after them Modred and his knights).

Glendower.

Ah, treachery base! Modred with his vile horde
Has seized the throne; of Arthur's land he's lord!
With all our courage we did fight—
Defend us now against the traitor's might!

(Modred and knights rush in.

Modred
(pursuing Glendower.
Away with him! I'll mete out your reward!
Seize him!

The Knights.

Hail to thee, Modred brave, our lord!
(Glendower and his warriors are forcibly led away; Modred and knights exeunt.

Glendower
(behind the scene.
Merlin! Merlin!

EIGHTH SCENE.

Merlin

(who has stood as though stunned, starts, staggers a few paces and falls down upon the steps of the temple.

Woe! The token!
By you my strength was broken!
Prophetic power I have lost
Since love this garden's entrance crossed!

Vivien
(approaches him with fear.
Beloved!

Merlin.

Unhappy thou!
(Lost in brooding.
Such was my harp's true warning!
I felt its force—yet treated it with scorning!
Oh God! forgive my wicked crime!
To render holiest service thou did'st send me;
Thou raisest thy servant above mortals sublime;
Against delusive lust defend me,
And with your precious love befriend me!
(To Vivien.
Farewell, I shudder while those words I'm speaking!
But—no—'tis impossible—Oh, farewell!

Vivien.

You say farewell?

Merlin.

Farewell—Go, other pleasures seeking.

Vivien
(in terror.
You bid me go?

Merlin
(with violent emotion.
I must—farewell!

MERLIN.

Zu wilden Manneskämpfen hin
Zog mich ein eitler Heldensinn!
Ich bleibe Dein! Was ist mir Näh' und
    Ferne,
Da doch die Liebe nimmer mich ver-
    lässt!
Ja, wie der Himmel festhält seine Sterne,
So halt' ich Dich, o Du Geliebte, fest!

(Die Sonne geht unter; Merlin und Viviane sitzen in ruhiger Umarmung da und sehen einander entzückt in's Auge. Geschrei und Tumult hinter der Scene.

Stimmen
              (hinter der Bühne.
Merlin! Merlin!

(Der Tumult wächst an. Hereinbrechende Nacht. Der Mond, bald hellleuchtend, bald von Wolken verdeckt.

Merlin.
Welch' ein Getös? Wer ruft mir?

Glendower
             (hinter der Scene.
O schütze mich, Merlin!

SIEBENTE SCENE.

(Glendower und einige Krieger stürzen herein, gleich darauf Modred und Ritter.)

Glendower.
Verrath, Merlin! Modred mit seinem
    Tross
Raubt Artus' Thron, besetzt ist Stadt
    und Schloss!
Wir wehrten uns mit Kraft und Muth,
Vergebens war's, schütz' uns vor seiner
    Wuth!

(Modred und viele Ritter stürzen herein.

Modred
             (Glendower nachstürzend.
Hinweg mit ihm! Dir wird dein Lohn zu
    Theil —
Greift ihn!

Die Ritter.
Heil Modred! König Modred Heil!
(Glendower und die Krieger werden gewaltsam hinweggeführt; Modred und die Ritter ab.

Glendower
             (hinter der Scene.
Merlin! Merlin!

ACHTE SCENE.

Merlin
(der während dieses ganzen Vorgangs starr, keines Wortes mächtig, dagestanden, fährt jetzt auf, taumelt einige Schritte und sinkt an den Stufen des Tempels nieder.

Weh! — Betrogen!
Der Fürst durch mich belogen!
Mein Seheraug' ist mir geraubt:
Die Gnade wich von meinem Haupt.

Viviane
             (nähert sich ihm furchtsam.
Geliebter!

Merlin
             (sich erhebend.
Unseliges Weib —
(Er bleibt in Sinnen versunken stehen.
Das also war's! — Das war der Harfe
    Mahnung?
Das sah mein Aug' in letzter Seher-
    ahnung?
O Herr, vergieb mir meine Schuld!
Zu heiligem Dienste hast du mich ge-
    sendet,
Vor allen Sterblichen erhob mich deine
    Huld:
Und ich, zu eiter Lust gewendet,
Ich hab' mein eig'nes Aug' geblendet!
    (Zu Viviane.
Leb' wohl, — ein Schauer strömt durch
    meine Glieder —
Doch, — nein! Ich kann nicht anders, —
    lebe wohl!

Viviane.
Was sagtest Du?

Merlin.
Leb' wohl, — Du siehst mich niemals
    wieder.

Viviane
             (starr vor Entsetzen.
Was sagtest Du?

Merlin
             (in heftiger Bewegung.
Ich muss — leb' wohl!

Vivien.
Beloved husband! Can you go away!

Merlin.
Upon myself I've brought this sorrow!
Where shall I ever forgiveness borrow!
Lord, give me strength—farewell, I cannot stay!

Vivien.
You mean to desert me?

Merlin.
In its own fire my love must burn!
To holy duties I must return!
Before my last remaining strength you've sapped
These bonds of passion must by me be broken,
And every loving thought remain unspoken—
I must forget whatever here has happed!

Vivien.
Beloved! speak and quell my fearing!
Oh tell me—what then have I done!

Merlin.
Woe's me! while I the voice of love was hearing,
King Arthur's Sovereignty was gone!
(Deeply moved.
Farewell, my love! Oh, I have loved you well;
Farewell, my wife! Go where bright pleasures bloom,
I stay to meet my dreaded doom!

Vivien
(wildly embracing him.
No! No! My lover, you must not leave me,
Close to my throbbing heart I'll hold you,
You must not, shall not, cannot leave me,
So close unto my breast I fold you!
And must I then lose my happiness
In one short hour? My direst foe
Could do no worse—Let your caress
Assure me that from me you ne'er will go!

Merlin.
Away I must, although with grief I die;
Farewell—alas, I dare not linger nigh!

Vivien
(with growing wildness
Here I will hold you,
Ever caress you,
Forever enfold you,
Never release you!
Thus I twine myself around you!
Thus—with my passion I have bound you!
And never I'll leave you. I would rather slay!
Fear me! Fear the Huntress wild for her prey!

Merlin.
I must—farewell!

Vivien.
Lover, be true!

Merlin.
I must away, for God himself is calling!

Vivien
(sinking down.
Here, lying at your feet, I pray you!

Merlin.
I must!—

Vivien.
Oh stay!

Merlin.
My God himself is calling!

Vivien.
Ha!
(She jumps up and seizes the magic veil.
Never, no, never, shall you leave me!

(She throws the veil over him. A terrific clap of thunder. Sudden change of scene. The temple remains. All else is a rocky wilderness. On a rock where was the knoll, lies Merlin, half recumbent chained to the rock with fiery glowing chains. Upon a rock opposite him appears the mocking demon.)

Viviane.
Geliebter Mann! Du gehst von mir?

Merlin.
Hab' ich die Schuld auf mich geladen:
Ich muss zurück zum Quell der Gnaden! —
Herr, gieb mir Kraft! — Leb' wohl! Ich geh' von Dir!

Viviane.
Verlassen willst Du mich?

Merlin.
So zertret' ich mein eigenes Glück!
Zu heiligem Dienst muss ich zurück!
Eh' Du noch meine letzte Kraft gebannt,
Zerbrechen muss ich Deine Zauberketten —
Und nun hinweg! Den König muss ich retten,
Noch schwing ich sie, die starke Zauberhand!

Viviane.
Geliebter, was ist mein Verschulden?
O sag' mir, was hab' ich gethan?

Merlin.
Unsel'ge! mehr, als Du, werd' ich erdulden,
Um meines Glückes kurzen Wahn!
(heftig erschüttert.
Leb' wohl, leb' wohl! — O ich hab' Dich geliebt! —
Geh' hin, wo's selige Menschen giebt!
Leb' wohl mein Weib! Zu Sterblichen geh' hin,
Die nicht so elend, wie Merlin.

Viviane
(ihn wild umschlingend.
Nein! nein! Du darfst mich nicht verlassen,
Ich halte mich an Deinem Busen fest,
So will ich ewig Dich umfassen,
Bis dass mein Leben mich verlässt!
So büssen soll ich mein kurzes Glück?
Die Eine Stunde? Merlin! Merlin!
O sag' mir's nur mit einem Blick:
So, Theurer, so wirfst Du mich nicht dahin?!

Merlin.
Ich muss! o soll ich in Jammer vergeh'n?
Leb wohl! ich darf Dich nicht mehr seh'n!

Viviane.
(mit immer steigender Wildheit.
Ich will Dich halten,
Will Dich umschlingen,
Mit allen Gewalten
Will ich Dich zwingen!
So — wind' ich mich um Deinen Leib!
Fürchte, fürchte das wüthende Weib!
Ich lasse Dich nicht. — Ich tödte Dich, Merlin!
Fürchte, fürchte die wilde Jägerin!

Merlin.
Ich muss — lass ab!

Viviane.
Geliebter Mann!

Merlin.
Ich muss dahin, wohin mich Gott erkoren!

Viviane
(niederfallend.
Zu Deinen Füssen fleh' ich Dich an!

Merlin.
Ich schwör's!

Viviane.
Halt ein!

Merlin.
Beim Himmel sei's geschworen!

Viviane.
Ha!
(Sie springt auf und ergreift den Schleier.
Nimmer, nimmer verlässest Du mich!

(Sie hat bei den letzten Worten den Schleier über sein Haupt geworfen. Furchtbarer Donnerschlag. Die Scene ist verwandelt. Im Vordergrunde der Tempel, wie früher sonst öde Felsenlandschaft. Auf einem Felsen, an der Stelle der Anhöhe, liegt Merlin, halb aufgerichteten Leibes, mit feurig-glühenden Ketten angeschmiedet. Der Mond leuchtet hell über seinem Haupte. Der Dämon erscheint auf einem Felsen, Merlin gegenüber, mit wildem Lachen. Viviane, die vom Momente der Katastrophe starr vor Entsetzen, wie betäubt, stehen geblieben war, fährt nun beim Lachen des Dämon jäh empor, wendet sich, erblickt Merlin am Felsen und stürzt mit einem erschütternden Schrei zu Boden. — Der Vorhang fällt.

(Ende des zweiten Aktes.)

THIRD ACT.

(Scene as at the end of the preceding act. Thick clouds envelope the background; only a few jagged rocky points penetrate them. In the foreground to the left is the temple, to the right a huge rock, forming at its foot a kind of stone bench. Morning.)

FIRST SCENE.

Vivien.

(at the rock to the right; alone, in half recumbent posture).

(in a low, melancholy voice.

The grey of morning? Woe! Eternal
    night!
Come, gentle sleep, and close my weary
    eye!
I've watched throughout the darkness to
    the light,
What help is there? Oh would that I
    might die!
I've weeping prayed that God would end
    this drear
Existence. Death, alas, would welcome
    be!
Will Heaven ne'er my supplication hear
And never to my prayer responsive be!

(She wearily sinks back into slumber. Morgana rises in a bright light and approaches Vivien.)

SECOND SCENE.

MORGANA. VIVIEN.

Morgana.

The enchanted calmness of my home
    was broken
By weeping loud; I heard your woeful
    call,
Unhappy woman fair! Had I not
    spoken
Unto the demon! He held me in his
    thrall.
How pale you are! You move my pity
    deep.
        (steps nearer to her.
Sleep on! But hear my message while
    you sleep.
Know you, child, from whence I came?
There is neither grief nor shame;
Scented airs float o'er the Ice,
And the dew gleams brilliantly.
Heaven's brightness gladden you,
Purest dews enliven you!
May the breezes soft and warm
Gently waft you from all harm!

(Vivien makes a gesture toward Morgana and smiles in her dream.)

She moves! She smiles! Forgotten is
    her fear!
She dreams of some good spirit near!

Vivien.

        (dreaming.)
A golden light! And you so fair and
    bright,
Who are you that dispel the night?

        (Seeks to raise herself.

Morgana.

        (spreading her hands over her.
Slumber, maiden, peacefully!
Heed Morgana's prophecy!
Though your eyes are dim with weeping
Let your heart this hope be keeping!
When on the deciding day
The destroyer claims his prey;
Love, that's stronger far than death,
Triumph shall o'er powers evil.
Love, that's stronger far than death,
Shall with your expiring breath
Triumph even o'er the devil.

III. AKT.

(Scene, wie am Schluss des vorigen Aktes. Dichte Wolken verhüllen den Hintergrund, aus dem nur einige spitze Felsenzacken hervorblicken. Im Vordergrunde links der Tempel; rechts ein mächtiger Felsblock, der unten eine Art Steinbank bildet. Morgen.)

ERSTE SCENE.

(Viviane am Felsen, rechts; allein, halbliegend.)

Viviane
(dumpf und leise.

Graut schon der Morgen? Diese ew'ge Nacht!
Müd' ist mein Aug'. — Schlaf ein, mein Aug', schlaf ein —
Ich hab' die ewige Finsterniss durchwacht:
Was frommt's? was soll's? Schlaf ein, für immer ein.
Ich hab' geweint in brünstigstem Gebet —
Was frommt's? Verschlossen ist des Himmels Huld!
Ich hab' kein Heil, hab' keine Gnad' erfleht
Für meine Qualen und für meine Schuld?
(Sie lehnt das Haupt matt zurück und entschlummert. Morgana steigt in einem hellen Lichtschein herauf und nähert sich ihr langsam.)

ZWEITE SCENE.

MORGANA. VIVIANE.

Morgana.

Aus heil'ger Ruh' weckt mich die tiefste Klage
Stark, wie kein Zauberruf mir je erklang!
Unseliges, holdes Weib! O Fluch dem Tage,
Da jener Dämon mich zur Botschaft zwang!
Wie bleich Du bist! die Seele rührst Du mir.
(Sie tritt zu ihr hin.
Schlummre, — doch hör': denn Tröstung bring ich Dir.
Weisst Du, Kind, woher ich kam?
Da ist Trauer nicht, noch Gram;
Süsser Duft ob lichter Au,
Und im Glanze perlt der Thau.
Himmlisch Licht umschwebe Dich,
Heller Thau belebe Dich!
Sel'ge Lüfte, lind und warm,
Lösen, lösen Deinen Harm!
(Viviane macht eine Bewegung nach Morgana hin, lächelt im Traum, und streckt die Arme nach ihr.
Sie regt sich — lächelt. Tief in bangem Weh'
Ahnt sie schon guten Geistes Näh'! —

Viviane
(träumend.

Welch gold'nes Licht! — Und Du, so schön und mild,
Wer bist Du, leuchtendes Gebild? —
(Sie will sich aufraffen.

Morgana
(die Hände über sie breitend.

Schlummre, Mägdlein, schlummre fort!
Hör' Morgana's Seherwort!
Wie Dich Schuld und Jammer quäle:
Tröste, tröste Deine Seele!
Wenn am dunklen Scheidepfad
Jauchzend der Verderber naht:
Liebe, stärker, als der Tod,
Wird des Unheils Mächte zwingen —
Liebe, stärker, als der Tod,
Wird in tiefster Herzensnoth
Ew'ges Heil dem Freund erringen!

MERLIN.

Vivien.
(dreaming.
What's the music I hear sounding?
Can you, evil powers confounding,
Shatter Merlin's glowing chains.

Morgana.
I cannot aid—I but foretell,
Love at last the victory gains,
Broken is the power of hell!
(vanishes.

Vivien.
(awakens.
Where are you? 'Twas a dream!
(Vivien's maidens enter from the left.

Chorus of Maidens.
Must you forever tarrying here
Pass all your hours in darkness drear?
Oh come with us your comrades so true!—
We'll love you, caress you, and frolic with you!
Come where the forest so long does mourn you!
Wind on your horn the merriest tune:
While we with blushing roses adorn you!
Bloom with the blooming roses of June!
Oh let not the roses mourn you!

Vivien.
What was I dreaming?

Chorus.
Speak, did you dream?

Vivien.
A goddess fair and bright I saw,
Her message I heard, and hope did gleam.

Chorus.
Tell us the message!

Vivien.
I know it no more
Forgotten 'tis, a fading gleam,
Yet o'er me it floats like a heavenly dream.

Chorus.
Oh may this token now gladden your heart,
Stay here no longer!
(tumult behind the scenes.
Oh swiftly depart!
(renewed tumult.

Vivien.
The day breaks now, and there so near!
Destroys ye my sight! Away from here!
I cannot remain here—I cannot go!
Loved Merlin! I cannot behold you so!

Chorus.
Come, beloved mistress, no more remain!

Vivien.
Oh mourn with me, sisters, and share my pain!
(She sinks into their arms. They gently lead her to the left. The clouds lift; Merlin is seen for a while at the rock.)

THIRD SCENE.

Merlin.
(after a pause
Now risest thou in golden glory bright!
The lark is singing its joyous lay:
Still 'round me hover the spirits of night,
Mockingly greeting me, their prey—
Retreat now, ye shadows! Oh grant me the light,
Oh hide not the comforting rays from my sight!
(Spirits hovering around Merlin in dense clouds.

With mockery your prayer we greet,
'Tis as your master willed!
Your pain to him is pleasure most sweet,
Thus knows he his wish is fulfilled!

MERLIN.

Viviane
(wie oben.
Welche Töne hör' ich klingen!
Kannst Du Unheils Macht bezwingen:
Löse, löse seine Noth!

Morgana.

Schauen kann ich — nicht vollbringen;
Liebe, stärker, als der Tod,
Wird ihm ew'ges Heil erringen!
(Versinkt.

Viviane
(erwachend.
Wo bist Du? — Welch' ein Traum?!
(Vivianens Jungfrauen kommen von der linken Seite.

Chor der Jungfrauen.

Hast Du am Felsen so lang gewacht?
Willst Du hier trauern Tag und Nacht?
O komm mit uns, o weile nicht hier —
Wir kosen, wir singen, wir spielen mit Dir!
Komm! wollen wir jauchzend die Wälder durchtosen?
Jagdspies und Hörner liegen bereit:
Winden wir Kränze? Pflücken wir Rosen?
O komm, es ist die Rosenzeit!

Viviane.

Was hab' ich geträumt?

Chor.

Sprich, welch ein Traum?

Viviane.

Sah eine Göttin, licht und hehr —
Kunde vernahm ich — ich fass' es kaum —

Chor.

Sprich, welche Kunde?

Viviane.

Ich weiss es nicht mehr.
Vergessen ist's — entschwunden ganz.
Doch liegt's über mir, wie himmlischer Glanz —

Chor.

Freu' Dich des Zeichens! es deutet Dir Heil.

Doch weile nicht hier —
(Tumult hinter der Scene.
O Herrin, enteil'!
Hörst Du es brausen? Dort tobt die Schlacht:
Fürst Artus kämpft mit Modred's Macht —
(Erneuerter Tumult.

Viviane.

Der Tag bricht an — und dort! o dort!
Erblindet, ihr Augen! Ja fort! schnell fort!
Ich kann nicht bleiben — ich kann nicht geh'n:
Geliebter! — so — soll ich dich wiedersehn?

Chor.

Komm, traute Herrin, weile nicht hier!

Viviane.

O trauert, ihr Schwestern, trauert mit mir!
(Sie sinkt dem Chor in die Arme, der sie mit sanfter Gewalt nach der linken Seite wegführt. Die Wolken verziehen sich. Merlin am Felsen wird für eine Weile ganz sichtbar.

DRITTE SCENE.

Merlin
(nach einer Pause.

Nun steigst Du herauf, Du goldene Pracht!
Dort flattert die Lerche jauchzend empor:
Nur mich umschweben die Geister der Nacht,
Höhnender Sang raunt mir in's Ohr —
O weichet, ihr Schatten! o gönnt mir das Licht,
Verhüllt mir die Strahlen, die tröstenden nicht!

Geisterchor
(in dichten Wolken Merlin umschwebend.

Wir spotten Dein, wir lachen Dein,
So hat es der Meister gewollt!
Knirschen sollst Du in Jammer und Pein,
Dein Knirschen es tönt ihm so hold!

Lancelot
(mit mehreren Rittern und Kriegern kommt von der rechten Seite.)

Lancelot.

(With several knights and warriors enters from the right.)
Ho! Merlin! Where is he?

Merlin.

(Up to his breast in clouds, so that his chains are invisible.)
Who calls?

Lancelot.

His voice now hear we! This region so dark,
These thickening clouds! Once more, now hark!

Merlin.

Oh day of sorrow!

Lancelot.

Hear, Merlin, hear!
This our last day of freedom will be!
With a twofold foe King Arthur fights—
A savage boar he storms through the fray;
The Saxons have joined Modred's base knights,
Against such numbers we'll lose the day.
Hence hither has King Arthur sent me:
If once a traitorous sprite did blind thee,
That treachery base thou did'st not know;
Arise and save us. Stamp out our double foe!
Arouse thyself! In vain King Arthur's coping
With treachery base. For thy strong help he's hoping.

Chorus of Knights.

Arouse thyself and trample the foe
With whom our gallant king is coping!

Merlin.

Almighty God! In vain King Arthur's hoping!
(enter Gawain and several Knights.

Gawain.

The King has sent for thee. Cursed be this day!
The warriors flee—he seeks death in the fray.
Where are you, Merlin? Thy aid yet remains!

Merlin

My land? My King! I am bound in chains!
(He tugs furiously at his chains.

Lancelot and Chorus of Warriors.

Arise, mighty Merlin! Our strength thou hast been;
Far, far in our van shalt thou be seen!
Thou often hast rescued us in war,
With thee invincibles we are;
Lead us, lead us! Once more we will hope
Victorious with our foes to cope!

Lancelot.

There but be seen; anew rage the fight!
Our men trust firmly in thy might.

Chorus.

Lead us Merlin! Thy strength still remains.

Merlin.

(as above.
In chains, in chains, in devilish chains!
(The clouds lift; the fiery chains are seen.

Lancelot.

(seeing the chains.
He in chains! Ha! What do we see!

Merlin.

Come death! Come death!

Lancelot.

Away must we!
Oh woe my king! My land, oh woe!
Your mighty Merlin's fallen low.
(They retreat in terror.

Chorus.

Why halts the seer? Oh woe! Oh woe!

Lancelot.

Come and meet death! His shame you shall know.
(They turn to depart.

MERLIN.

Lancelot.

Merlin? wo ist er?

Merlin
(bis an die Brust dicht von den Nebeln umflossen so dass die Ketten unsichtbar sind).

Wer ruft?

Lancelot.

Dort seine Stimme! — Welch düsterer Raum,
Welch dichtes Gewölk! — ich seh' Dich kaum —

Merlin.

O Tag des Jammers!

Lancelot.

Hör' mich, Merlin!
Heut' fällt der Briten Freiheit dahin! —
Fürst Artus kämpft mit doppeltem Feind —
Ein wilder Eber, durchstürmt er die Schlacht:
Die Sachsen sind mit Modred vereint,
Und wir erliegen der Uebermacht.
Drum hat der König mich gesendet:
Wenn Dich ein tückischer Geist geblendet,
Dass Du des Elenden Schuld verkannt:
Erhebe Dich nun — errette Fürst und Land!
Erhebe Dich! bald ist Alles verloren!
Bei Deiner Treue sei beschworen!

Chor der Ritter.

Erhebe Dich! rette Fürst und Land!
Bei Deiner Treue sei beschworen!

Merlin.

Allmächtiger! O wär' ich nie geboren!
(Gawein mit einigen Rittern kommt.

Gawein.

Mich sendet der König! O Tag der Noth!
Die Mannen weichen — der König sucht den Tod —
Wo bist Du, Merlin! Nur Du kannst retten!

Merlin.

Mein Volk! mein Fürst! — ha, Ketten! Ketten!
(Er zerrt wüthend an den Fesseln.

Lancelot und Chor der Krieger.

Auf, mächtiger Seher! Hilf uns, Merlin!
Du sollst an unserer Spitze zieh'n!
Du halfest oft in Kampf und Krieg, —
Wo Du erscheinst, da ist der Sieg!
Führ' uns, führ' uns! Dann hoffen wir wieder,
Du wirfst all' unsre Feinde nieder!

Lancelot.

Zeige Dich nur! Erneu're die Schlacht!
Sie glauben fest an deine Macht!

Chor.

Führ' uns, Merlin! Nur Du kannst retten!

Merlin.
(wie oben.

Ha, Ketten! Ketten! höllische Ketten!
Die Wolken zerstreuen sich, die Ketten werden rothglühend sichtbar.

Lancelot.
(die Ketten erblickend.

In Ketten! — ha! was ist gescheh'n!

Merlin.

Den Tod! Den Tod!

Lancelot.

Kommt, lasst uns geh'n!
Stirb hin, mein Fürst! mein Volk, sink' hin!
So fiel Dein herrlicher Merlin!
(Alle weichen entsetzt zurück.

Chor.

Wehe! Wehe! Was ist gescheh'n!

Lancelot.

Kommt in den Tod! Die Schmach sollt ihr nicht seh'n!
(Sie wenden sich zum Abgehen

Merlin.

They go! They go! I must follow the brave!
O God! wilt not some pity have?
(He tugs furiously at his chains.
I must follow them and break my chain!
O God! have pity on my pain!
These chains I must sunder—King Arthur is coping
With treachery, and for my aid is hoping;
How, if hell's power would make me free,
I would be damned for eternity!

The Demon.

(coming swiftly forward.
So be it then!
(A thunder clap. Darkness; the chains fall. Lancelot, Gawain and the Knights start back with a loud cry.)

Demon.

(Out of the darkness.
Triumphant is my might!
(vanishes.
(It is bright day again. The scene changes to Merlin's magic garden as in act second; Vivien with her maidens appears in the left on the knoll and looks terrified about her; then she hastens toward Merlin, who stands, pale and drawn up to his full height, in the middle of the stage.)

Vivien.

All hail my beloved? Oh heavenly light!
(She sinks down at his feet.

Merlin.

My wife! Oh my beloved wife!
(He raises her.

Vivien.

And dare I feel that I am shriven?
Forgive you me?

Merlin.

(With deep emotion.
Were I but so forgiven!
(He rouses himself from his brooding.)

Now let what must be wrought on me!
Await me here!
Here meet me after bloody victory!
Away!
(He seizes a sword from one of the warriors and brandishes it on high.)
I lead!

Lancelot. Gawain. Knights and warriors.

Lead on!
(Exeunt all except Vivien and her maidens.

FOURTH SCENE.

Vivien.

Shine out, bright summits, with verdure glowing,
For the day of rapture is here!
Tremble, ye forests, ye roses blowing—
For the day of rapture is here!
Earth, cover yourself with your gayest green,
Sing all sweet birds both far and near!
Blossom and sing, in sweet Love's demesne!
For the day of rapture is here!
(The maidens joyously surround Vivien.

Vivien.

Wreathe me, oh sisters, with garlands enfolden!
Gather red roses, and yellow, for me!
Glow with the crimson, gleam with the golden,
Ringlets, my ringlets, in beauty free!
Over pathways bestrewn with flowers
Hither to me my lover returns,
Proud in the triumph of all his powers,
He for whom every bosom yearns!
(Her maidens adorn her hair and bosom with flowers.)

Vivien.

Say, am I lovely? and will he loving be?
Ah, bitter tears were flowing so free!
Can he traces of sorrow still see?
Say, will my cheek still pallid be?
If, like a flower, I could unfold me,

MERLIN.

Merlin.
O bleibt doch, bleibt! Herr, hab' Erbarmen!
Seht, ich zersprenge sie mit meinen Armen!
(Er versucht wüthend die Ketten zu zerreissen.
Sie gehen, — ich muss — ich muss ihnen nach.
O Gott! blick her auf meine Schmach!
Ich muss euch zersprengen — ich muss, ihr Ketten!
Frei muss ich sein — mein Volk muss ich erretten:
Und wär' es die Hölle, die mich befreit!
Und sollt ich verdammt sein in Ewigkeit!

Der Daemon
(plötzlich mit starken Schritten aus dem Hintergrunde vortretend.
Es sei!
(Donnerschlag. Dichte Finsterniss; die Ketten fallen klirrend ab. Lancelot, Gawein und die Ritter wenden sich mit lautem Aufschrei zurück.

Daemon
(aus der Finsterniss.
Mein ist der Sieg! Vollbracht! Vollbracht!
(Versinkt.
(Es ist wieder heller Tag; die Scene ist verwandelt: Merlins Rosengarten, wie im zweiten Aufzug: Viviane mit ihren Jungfrauen erscheint links auf der Anhöhe und blickt voll Shrecken um sich; dann eilt sie auf Merlin zu, der in der Mitte der Bühne bleich, hochaufgerichtet dasteht.)

Viviane.
Geliebter! Geliebter! O himmlische Macht!
(Sie sinkt ihm zu Füssen.

Merlin.
Mein Weib! o mein geliebtes Weib!
(Er richtet sie auf.

Viviane.
Darf ich den Blick zu Dir erheben?
Vergiebst Du mir?

Merlin
(in tiefster Erschütterung.
Wär' so auch *mir* vergeben!
(Er rafft sich aus dumpfen Sinnen je auf.

Ha! mag denn, was da will, gescheh'n!—
Hier harre mein!
Nach blut'gem Sieg sollst Du mich wiederseh'n!
Nun auf!
(Er nimmt von einem der Krieger ein Schwert and schwingt es hoch.
Mir nach! —

Lancelot, Gawein, Ritter und Krieger.
Dir nach!
(Alle ausser Viviane und den Jungfrauen ab.

VIERTE SCENE.

Viviane.
Blüht auf, ihr Felsen! ihr Büsche erblühet!
Denn der Tag der Wonne ist da!
Ergrünet, ihr Bäume, — ihr Rosen erglühet!
Denn der Tag der Wonne ist da!
Decke dich, Erde, mit freudigem Grün,
Singet, ihr Vögel, fern und nah',
Alles soll singen, Alles soll blüh'n:
Denn der Tag der Wonne ist da!
(Die Jungfrauen haben sich freudig um Viviane gesammelt.

Viviane.
Schmückt mich, o Schwestern, — schmückt mich, Ihr Holden!
Gelbröslein, Rothröslein pflückt mir vom Hag!
Schmückt mir die Locken rosig und golden,
Dass ich in Schönheit prangen mag!
Denn auf blumenbestreueten Wegen
Kehrt mir bald der Geliebte zurück,
Denn dem Geliebten zieh' ich entgegen,
Jauchzend in seinem und meinem Glück!
(Die Jungfrauen pflücken überall Blumen ab und schmücken ihr Busen und Haar.

Viviane.
Sagt, bin ich schön? und wird er mich lieben?
Ach, meine Thränen flossen so reich!
Ist nicht der Thränen Spur geblieben?
Und ist mir nicht die Wange bleich?
O könnt' ich strahlen! könnt' ich prangen,

If in my blooming I could appear!
Then to his quickening breast he'd hold
   me,
For the day of rapture is here?

Chorus of Women.
(while Vivien is being adorned.
Yes, you are fair? And he will love
   you—
In grace and beauty rich you are!
You shine like the glowing sun above
   you,
Nor did your tears your beauty mar.
Now like a flower you are unfolding;
In all your blooming you'll appear!
Soon you to his breast will be folding—
For the day of rapture is here!
(The maidens ascend a little knoll to the left
and look eagerly toward the right.)

Vivien.
Look now, oh sisters! Is not he in
   sight?
Shine not the lances in glorious light?

The Virgins.
There's naught to see.

Vivien.
I 'gin to fear—
How long that he does not appear!
Oh angelic hosts descending
And my Merlin's life defending
With your swift ethereal lightness
Hover 'round him ever near;
Bring me back his longed-for bright-
   ness,
For his loved one waits in fear.
Like the dews of springtide stealing
To our hearts with gentle feeling,
So to me in kindness turning
He my sin may pardon quite!
May I ever bloom with yearning
In the rapture of his sight!

The Maidens.
They're coming! They're coming!

Vivien.
Rejoice! Oh rejoice! O happy meet-
   ing!
The day of rapture, of rapture is here!

FUNERAL MARCH.

Vivien.
My God, what sound!

FIFTH SCENE.

(Arthur, Gawain, Lancelot enter followed by
knights and warriors bearing Merlin on a bier.)

Arthur.
Here let us halt in his home of glory!
Long live Merlin's fame in story!
But we, alas, must mourn the brave!
   (pointing to the bier.
For with his life he did us save!

Vivien.
(Falls with a loud cry upon Merlin.
Woe, he is dead! Beloved one—beloved
   one!

Merlin.
   (opens his eyes.
My wife—'tis you! Oh lovely face!
(He spreads out his arms and slowly rises;
then embraces her.)
Oh lovely form no other can replace!
I see you once again in life!
You ne'er must leave me more, my love,
   my wife!
Let me not perish—still with me re-
   main—
Oh firmly clasp me; heaven will be
   your gain!

Vivien
   (choking with tears.
You shall not die!

Merlin.
Oh Vivien mine, I hold you!
In all your beauty to my heart I fold
   you—
Life, life! How often in the fray
Have I braved death unflinching, ever
   fearless!
Now that you love me I must pass away,
For death will not grant me with you to
   stay,
O God! let me not die in sorrow peer-
   less!
See there! See there!

Wie man kein Weib noch prangen sah!
Denn den Herrlichsten soll ich umfangen,
Denn der Tag der Wonne ist da!

Chor der Frauen
(während sie geschmückt wird.

Ja, Du bist schön! Er'wird Dich lieben—
In Huld und Schönheit prangst Du reich!
Nicht ist der Thränen Spur geblieben!
Du leuchtest ja, der Sonne gleich!
Die Freude strahlt auf Deinen Wangen,
Wie man kein Weib noch prangen sah!
Geh' hin, den Herrlichsten zu umfangen —
Denn der Tag der Wonne ist da!

(Die Jungfrauen waren auf eine kleine Erhöhung links gestiegen und blicken eifrig nach der rechten Seite.

Viviane.
Späht doch, Ihr Schwestern! kommt er noch nicht?
Blinken nicht Lanzen im goldenen Licht?

Die Jungfrauen.
Noch nichts zu seh'n!

Viviane.
Währt es noch lang'?
Kommt er noch nicht? fast wird mir bang!
Kommt herab, ihr Engelschaaren,
Meinen Trauten zu bewahren!
Mit dem schneeigen Gefieder
Hüllet mir ihn sorglich ein;
Bringet mir den Liebsten wieder,
Denn die Liebe harret sein.
Gleich dem Thau im Lenzgefilde
Giesst in's Herz ihm Gnad' und Milde,
Dass er sich zur Liebsten wende
Und vergesse ihre Schuld:
Dass ich blühe ohne Ende
In dem Glanze seiner Huld!

Die Jungfrauen.
Sie kommen! sie kommen!

Viviane.
Jauchzet, o jauchzet! Auf! ihm entgegen!
Der Tag der Wonne, der Wonne ist da!

(Trauermarsch aus der Ferne, immer näher kommend.

Viviane.
Gott! welche Töne!

FUENFTE SCENE.

(Artus, Gawein, Lancelot kommen; ihnen folgen Ritter und Krieger, Merlin auf einer Bahre tragend.)

Artus.

Hier haltet still an seinem Heiligthum:
Sein ist der Sieg, sein ist der Ruhm;
Doch unser ist das herbe Leid —

(Auf die Bahre deutend.

Um *solchen* Preis sind wir befreit!

Viviane
(die mit lautem Schrei zurückgefahren war, stürzt jetzt entsetzt auf Merlin.

Weh', ist er todt — Geliebter — Geliebter!

Merlin
(schlägt die Augen auf.

Mein Weib — Du bist's — Du holdes Haupt —

(Er breitet die Arme aus und erhebt sich langsam; dann umschliesst er sie heftig.

Der süsse Trost, ist er mir nicht geraubt?
Darf Dich mein Aug' noch einmal seh'n?
Mein Weib, mein Weib! lass mich nicht von Dir geh'n!
Lass mich nicht sterben, bleibe bei mir —
O halte mich fest: Der Himmel ist bei Dir!

Viviane
(in Thränen erstickt.

Du stirbst nicht!

Merlin.
Noch, noch halt' ich Dich umschlungen!
Das ist der Reiz, der meinen Sinn bezwungen —
O, leben! leben! Ach, in wildem Streit
Wie sprengt' ich oft in Tod und in Verderben!
Nun sterb' ich hin in tiefster Bitterkeit,
Mir naht der Tod in schrecklichstem Geleit:
O Gott, lass mich nicht in Verzweiflung sterben! —
O sieh, — sieh hin!

The Demon.

(In a fiery cloud on the summit of the rock.
Come! you are mine!

Arthur, Vivien, Chorus.

Apparition dread!

Merlin.

(Clinging to Vivien.
Woe! The destroyer! 'Twas he set me free!
He's come—the devil's minion I must be!

Demon.

(to Vivien.
Hence, wretched one!

Vivien.

Demon, I break your sway!
From me he never shall away!

Demon.

Let go, straightway!

Vivien.

Oh lofty prophetess,
Your comforting message I bless!
"When on the deciding day,
The destroyer claims his prey,
Love, that's stronger far than death,
Triumph shall o'er powers evil.
Love, that's stronger far than death,
Shall, with your expiring breath
Triumph even o'er the devil!"

Demon.

(to Merlin.
Now hence!

Vivien.

Away!

(to Merlin.
Now saved are we!
United ever we will be!
Your way, my way, your grave, my grave—
Then, the eternity we crave!
On earth I'll not remain alone;
So true as lives eternal love,
Our sins we both in death atone;
On wings of angels we'll float above—
Unto the hallowed regions of love!

(She draws a dagger and stabs herself.

Chorus.

What has she done?

Demon.

Curse heaven and earth!

Merlin.

(In dying stretches his arm out for Vivien.
Love, are you near?
Where are you? Loved one!

(He falls back and expires.

Vivien.

(sinking over him.
I'm here! I'm here!

Arthur and Chorus.

Heroic might, that lose we must,
Oh beauty bright, low in the dust!
Oh guide them, Love, most peacefully
To blessed immortality!

CURTAIN.

MERLIN.

Der Daemon
(war in einer feurigen Wolke auf der Felsenspitz erschienen.

Daemon.

Auf! Du bist mein!

Artus, Viviane, Chor.

Welch grauses Gebild!?

Merlin
(sich heftig an Viviane schliessend.

Weh! Der Verderber! Er hat mich befreit! —
In tiefster Pein, ihm hab' ich mich geweiht!

Daemon (zu Viviane.

Fort! elend Weib!

Viviane.

Unhold, rühr' ihn nicht an!
Kämpfst Du mit mir um diesen Mann?

Daemon.

Lass ab von ihm!

Viviane.

O Wort der Scherin,
Wie wachst Du auf in meinem Sinn!
Wenn am dunklen Scheidepfad
Grimmig der Verderber naht:
Liebe, stärker, als der Tod,
Wird des Unheils Macht bezwingen, —
Liebe, stärker, als der Tod —
Wird in tiefster Herzensnoth
Ew'ges Heil dem Freund erringen!

Daemon (zu Merlin.

Zu mir!

Viviane.

Hinweg! —
(zu Merlin.
Mein bist du, mein!
Dort, wo der Freund ist, will ich sein,
Dein Weg mein Weg, Dein Grab mein Grab —
In Ewigkeit lass ich von Dir nicht ab!
Auf Erden bleibe ich nicht allein!
So wahr die ewige Liebe lebt,
So wahr dies Licht am Himmel loht,
Schon fühl' ich den Fittig, der mich hebt, —
Mein bist Du im Tod, und nach dem Tod!
(Sie zieht einen Dolch und durchsticht sich.

Chor.

Was hast Du gethan?

Daemon.

Fluch Himmel und Erde!
(Versinkt.

Merlin
(richtet sich halb auf und streckt, brechenden Auges, wie suchend, die Arme nach Viviane).

O bist Du hier?
Wo bist Du? — Geliebte!
(Er sinkt zurück und stirbt.

Viviane
(an ihm niedersinkend.

Bei Dir! Bei Dir!

Artus. Chor.

O Heldenkraft, die uns entfliegt,
O Schönheit, die im Staube liegt!
Zum Frieden leite sie hinan,
O Liebe, die du obgesiegt!

Der Vorhang fällt.

ENDE.